From the Outside

From the Outside

Rethinking Church Doctrine

Tony Flannery

RED STRIPE PRESS

Published by
Red Stripe Press

an imprint of
Orpen Press
Upper Floor, Unit B3
Hume Centre, Hume Avenue
Park West Industrial Estate
Dublin 12
Ireland

email: info@orpenpress.com
www.orpenpress.com

Paperback ISBN 978-1-78605-102-8
ePub ISBN 978-1-78605-103-5

Printed in Dublin by SPRINTprint Ltd

Contents

Acknowledgements

This book is very much a product of my years away from public ministry, partly because I had the time to read, reflect and write. Over the past few years I had a number of fragments written, but little in the line of a coherent document. A phone call, followed by a meeting, with Michael Brennan of Red Stripe Press was the catalyst that gave me motivation and, even more importantly, a deadline. The coronavirus lockdown provided the peace and quiet necessary to do the rest. Therefore, I wish to acknowledge the major part Michael has played in the genesis of this book.

Fiona Biggs, with her long experience of publishing, and her knowledge of the religious world, was the perfect editor.

The managing editor, Eileen O'Brien, was meticulous in sorting out problems with the text and any anomalies in sentence construction. The number of occasions on which I got emails after midnight was an indication of Eileen's dedication to her profession.

A great many people encouraged me along the way, and to them all I am deeply grateful.

Lastly, I might acknowledge the part played by the Congregation for the Doctrine of the Faith. Without their intervention in my life neither this book nor my previous one, *A Question of Conscience*, would have seen the light of day.

Foreword

In 1947, the year Tony Flannery was born, Seán Ó Faoláin published *The Irish*, a thought-provoking reflection on our society. In the section on the Catholic Church, entitled 'The Priests', he claimed that the Church relied on 'the weapons of rigid authority' to proclaim its message. He asserted that intellectual debate was discouraged: 'One may be appalled to think that there is not in Ireland a single lay Catholic periodical to which one could apply the adjective enquiring, or even intelligent.'

He lamented the suspicion that existed between the Church and writers and intellectuals:

> *The tragedy of all this is, of course, that the priest and the writer ought to be fighting side by side if for nothing else than the rebuttal of the vulgarity that is pouring daily into the vacuum left in the popular mind by the dying out of the old traditional life. But there can be no such common ground as long as the priest follows the easy way of authority instead of discussion.*

Ó Faoláin was writing at a time when the power of the Catholic Church was at its zenith. It was a strictly disciplined and theologically and spiritually quiescent institution. It was a major player in education and health. Creative thinking and dialogue were frowned upon. Politicians feared the disapproval of the hierarchy.

Liam Ryan, one-time Professor of Sociology at Maynooth, judged that the then Church exuded 'four deadly sins, an obsession with sexual morality, clerical authoritarianism, anti-intellectualism or at best non-intellectualism, and a ghetto mentality'.

The dynamic and liberating Christian vision had been choked by infantile piety. Authority had slid into authoritarianism, charism had turned into control and humility had mutated into hubris. The law of love had been replaced by the love of law.

In the following decades this towering edifice crumbled due to social and economic change. In 1947 Ó Faoláin had discerned that the intellectual challenge was on the Church's doorstep and the Church was not up for it. It foundered as a new Ireland flourished.

After failure came scandal. In the 1990s the charnel room in the basement of the Church was prised open to reveal the Magdalen laundries, the mother-and-baby homes and the clerical and religious sexual abuse of children. It was followed by cover-ups and casuistic mental reservations that have left its credibility in tatters.

Tony Flannery was born when ecclesiastical pomp was pervasive, grew up in a Church wilting under cultural transformation, and has ministered in a broken one. The Second Vatican Council has been the guiding light of his ministry. It envisaged a Church willing to dialogue with modernity, a Church open to engaging with the insights of the secular world. Most of his ministry has been as a preacher of Redemptorist missions, mainly in Ireland, over four decades. Travelling from Malin to Mizen Head in the course of his work, he got a sense of Irish Catholicism, its strengths and its weaknesses, its hopes and aspirations, its hunger and its hurts. He was an engaging speaker and an innovative liturgist. On two occasions he gave missions in the community where I live, and he left a positive impression. His sermons were inspiring and leavened with humour. He gave fresh heart to those haunted by anguish in their lives. His articles in *Reality* magazine, an extension of his ministry, were stimulating and devoid of pious cliché.

In the Church, the 'glad confident morning' of the Second Vatican Council gave way to a long and dismal journey into night. During the papacies of John Paul II and Benedict XVI there was a retreat from the insights of the Council that had exhilarated so many Catholics. For Catholics whose lives had been shaped by the ideals of democracy, free speech and academic dialogue, the Church became an inhospitable place. Liberal clerics were silenced and a climate of fear enveloped theologians. In the words of English writer A.N. Wilson, the Congregation for the Doctrine of the Faith has 'ways of making you not talk'. As a result of articles questioning Church teaching on compulsory celibacy for priests, women's ordination and homosexuality, Tony experienced the heavy breath of Vatican disapproval. In 2012 he was banned from public ministry, an injustice that the Church has not yet rectified. He has borne his exclusion with grace and fortitude. He has devoted his time to reading and reflection. He has given his enquiring mind full rein. The fruits of his explorations on God, the theology of sexuality and Church governance are in this new book. He is uneasy with dogmatic formulations that do not admit to the possibility and value of new insights as humanity evolves. In parched terrain he has discovered new wells that are worthy of further exploration.

Now, read on ...

Kevin Hegarty
Priest and religious affairs commentator

Introduction

It has sometimes seemed to me that there are three weak stones settled
dangerously in the foundations of the modern church:
first, a government that excludes democracy;
second, a priesthood that minimises women;
third, a revelation that excludes future prophecy.

Teilhard de Chardin (died 1955)

Teilhard de Chardin was clearly a man ahead of his time, when you think that, back in the middle of the last century, and before the Second Vatican Council, he could so clearly see the issues that are now very much to the fore in our Church. The three aspects of Church life that he highlights are the issues that I broadly seek to explore in this book.

As I write, it is now almost nine years since the Congregation for the Doctrine of the Faith (CDF), the most powerful of the bodies that make up the Vatican government, set their sights on me, and informed the General Government of the Redemptorists that they regarded some of my writings as heretical. That led to almost a year of meetings and correspondence between my superiors and me, resulting in my being permanently withdrawn from ministry by the Redemptorists, under orders from the CDF. I was 65 years of age when that occurred and my book *A Question of Conscience*, published in 2013, gives a full account of the whole sorry saga. Since then, while remaining a priest and a Redemptorist, I have not exercised priestly ministry in public, with one notable exception, and I have by and large lived those years on the fringes of the institutional Church and the religious congregation.

The one exception was for my seventieth birthday, when I celebrated a public Mass in the hall of my native village of Attymon, County Galway. A further document from the CDF was conveyed to me recently with orders that I sign four specific statements, some of them similar to the original ones I was to sign, but also including new issues. Putting my name to these statements would be impossible for me, and I see this latest development being the final conclusion of my relationship with the Vatican, and the end to any possibility of me returning to active ministry. You will find this document in the Epilogue at the end of this book.

Being on the fringes of the Redemptorist congregation was largely my own choice, as I could have decided to continue living in the monastery and playing a role within the community. I considered this, but each day reminded me of the loss of ministry and, in the interest of my own well-being, I decided to move out, though I still have a warm relationship with my Redemptorist colleagues. Official Church policy was something over which I had no influence. I was not welcome to work as a priest in any diocese. As soon as I was 'withdrawn' from ministry Church doors were firmly closed so that I could no longer speak or exercise ministry in any Catholic church. In some ways, I can see all this as some form of gift, because I was forced to carve out a new niche for myself. Over the past eight years I have spoken publicly around Ireland, and in other countries, but only on one occasion on Catholic property. That happened in a parish in America where the priest openly violated a direct order from his bishop. In spite of all that, these have been very interesting and enlightening years for me. When the Association of Catholic Priests was invited to send delegates to an international Church reform meeting in Austria, I became involved in this movement, and in the process I have met a great variety of people. I have had time to read a lot, and have had a chance to reflect on faith, Church and my own life experience. I have talked and listened to many people. This book is to a fair extent the product of those years, and those encounters. I don't believe I could have written it if I had not gone through the experience of withdrawal/suspension, and the years that followed. Having lived most of my life immersed in Church affairs and ministry, standing back from it all at this time in my life gave me new perspectives, and both the freedom and the courage to pursue new ways of thinking. I think it is true to say that I am now a different person from the one who got that first phone call informing me of the

Vatican's interest in me. Around that time I came across a sentence that resonated with me: 'You must wait and see who you are when this thing is done with you.' My impression is that I have changed a good deal in these past years, and I hope this book will illustrate the nature of my changing ways of thinking and believing.

I know that these years have also been a time of great upheaval in the Catholic Church. Many people no longer practise their faith, and some have lost all belief in what the Church teaches. Indeed, for many people under the age of 60, the Church has no relevance at all. There are people who still believe in a spiritual dimension, who look beyond what is transient and connect with some form of divine presence in the world. Many are searching for new ways of understanding and, while still 'hanging in there' in terms of Church membership and practice, though maybe not as regularly as in the past, are struggling with acceptance of various Church structures and doctrines. I am hoping that this book might be helpful to people in these various stages of belief, unbelief and doubt. I have tried to open up new ways of looking at ancient doctrines that might make more sense to the modern mind, and make it easier for people to find meaning and purpose in their life and their faith.

I no longer believe that there is one set of doctrines that encompass the truth and that all other belief systems are false. Life is Mystery, and none of us can encompass the vastness of it; there is space and an open door for all, for those who are searching, for those whose faith does not pose any problems. I am not for a moment suggesting that I have the truth any more than others. The best any of us can do is get some glimpse of the mystery, and open ourselves to it in so far as we can recognise its working in our lives and in the world. If this book contains some insights that might help you on that journey, then my efforts will have been worthwhile.

1

We Are Where We Are, But How Did We Get Here?

Often I hear older priests, when asked publicly if, given a second chance, they would choose priesthood again, answering very positively that they would do it all again. Rarely is there a hint of regret, except from the occasional more outspoken one who might say that it would have been good to have married and had a family. When I am asked the question I am not at all sure of the answer. I am now 73 years of age and, inevitably, I reflect as I look back on my life. (Of course, apart from my own personal angle, the current crisis in priesthood and in the Church makes the question a very different one from what it was 55 years ago, when I first made my choice.) I went to a Redemptorist junior seminary at the age of twelve, and from there to a spiritual year in a novitiate when I completed my Leaving Cert at seventeen, and then on to the senior seminary.

I have no memory of any type of personal religious experience that might be classified as a direct call from God to religious life. When people have asked me about my 'vocation' I haven't quite known how to answer, since I am not at all sure what the word means. I can easily list a series of very human and practical reasons that might have contributed to the choice I made. Was it the very laudable ambition of my parents who, in a time of poverty and little opportunity for young people, wanted to ensure as best they could that I would have a reasonable chance of success and happiness? Was it the fact that I was the youngest of four children, all of whom spent some period of their lives in religious communities? As such, could it be said that I just followed their lead, rather than making any real personal decision?

I lived beside a Bord na Móna bog, which in the 1950s and 60s had a field of Nissen huts that housed workers. Transport wasn't freely available, so it was easier for some of the men to live on site. I am now aware that one of those huts housed what I suspect was a fairly rampant paedophile, and this man abused me sexually. I suspect he abused many other children, but at the time I thought I was the only one. It was not something that I discussed with any of my family or peers. I believe that this abuse did not destroy my life, but I acknowledge that it must have had some impact, and I am never quite sure how to measure the nature or the degree of its influence. Would it, subconsciously, have contributed to the choice of career I made? Or did I become a priest for a much simpler reason – the lack of any easily accessible secondary education, which meant that my brothers and I went to the Redemptorist school in Limerick, the junior seminary I referred to above, and I followed my brothers into the senior seminary. I must also accept that the religious belief system of the time had some influence. Priesthood was held up as the highest state in life, a higher religious state than marriage. Life in the world was portrayed as full of pitfalls, occasions of sin, mostly sexual sin, the consequence of which could be an eternity in hell. Priesthood offered a refuge from such perils. I do not find it easy to discern what exactly was going on in my mind in those early years, but I was probably afraid that if I did not become a priest I would not be able to manage the business of my eternal salvation. I am also inclined to think now that the experience of sexual abuse skewed my notions of sex and caused me to fear it. I had the feeling that where God was concerned, I just did not measure up, feelings of guilt being one of the standard consequences for people who are sexually abused as children. These possible explanations of my choice of priesthood are given with the benefit of hindsight and, as I write them, I am aware of how naive I was. Whatever the reasons or the influences that were at work, I have spent 56 years as a member of a religious order, and 46 of those years as an ordained priest of the Catholic Church, and while I had my ups and downs, as everybody does, I know that I have been blessed and privileged in so many ways.

When I think of the first year after I joined the Redemptorists, the novitiate as it was known, its structure, the philosophy and theology behind it, I realise how much has changed in the course of my lifetime. I think there is a country song that goes 'If I knew then what I know now I'd be a wiser man'. But I didn't. In fact I now see my young self as being very raw, fairly immature and relatively innocent. Looking back from a distance of over 50 years, the term I would use to sum up what was wrong with that novitiate year is 'life-denying'. We were locked away, not allowed outside the confines of the monastic enclosure except to go for walks as a group, not allowed television, radio or newspaper. Life has taught me that the most important thing we have to do is live life to the full and engage with it as deeply as we possibly can, according to our capacity for vivacity, for energy. The words of Jesus resonate: 'I have come that you may have life, and have it to the full.' If we are to grow into that fullness we need to learn the many lessons that life teaches us.

I went to the seminary in my late adolescence. Given that I had spent my early adolescence in a junior seminary it is unlikely that I successfully negotiated the tasks that Erik Erikson, the developmental psychologist, ascribes to this phase of life. Erikson defines adolescence as a crucial time when we struggle to form an identity. As we leave childhood, and before we attain adulthood, we have to find out who we are, what our values are, how we want to shape our lives. Erikson suggests that the two main areas to be explored during this period are sexuality and occupation. Living in a single-sex institution, largely cut off from all other life, was hardly the environment for any such exploration. There was little opportunity for reflecting on sexuality, given that it was presented to us as dangerous territory, and freedom to think and explore occupations was difficult since we were presumed to be already committed to life as priests and religious. Despite this, some of the more courageous among us did an assessment of themselves and of the system that enabled them to decide that priesthood was not for them.

In this tightly confined and controlled hothouse we were exposed to a spirituality that was negative and, more injurious than that, it imparted an image of God as someone who was distant, controlling and demanding, someone who could never be fully satisfied, someone who was to be feared. In my experience, it took a long time to undo the damage of that year. Happily for me, and for the rest of us, the Second Vatican Council came along and this led to more freedom of expression, to a more open attitude to literature and the arts. We were studying the Council documents and loving the new thinking we found in them. The world was to be embraced, not eschewed. The Church was not the building, it was not the hierarchical structure, it was the community of believers. By the time I was ordained the nature of the theology and spirituality we were getting had become much more positive. However, it took me many years to shed the guilt complex that those early years ingrained in me.

I have been in religious life since 1964, and a priest since 1974. I have lived through the collapse of the Irish Catholic Church, viewing it very much from the inside. In 1999 I wrote a book called *From the Inside*. Two years before that I had written my first book, called *The Death of Religious Life?* In that book I predicted that religious life, as we have known it and as it has flourished in Ireland for close on two centuries, was in rapid decline and would probably die out. In hindsight, this view was hardly a great sociological breakthrough. The signs were there for anyone who wanted to see.

During my student years in the 1960s the decay in male religious life and in vocations to the priesthood began to show itself fairly dramatically. When I joined the Redemptorists we had almost a hundred students studying for the priesthood in our seminary in Galway. By the time I was ordained ten years later, that number was somewhere in the twenties. During those ten years I witnessed the exodus of a great many young men, some brilliant and talented, others suffering from various forms of nervous collapse. They departed in great numbers. Looking back it is obvious why this happened. The 1960s was a period of economic growth in Ireland, courtesy of fresh thinking by people like T.K. Whitaker. After a long era of stagnation, with the economic war of the 1930s, the Second World War and its aftermath of rationing, there was the beginning of an openness to the world in the late 1950s, which blossomed in the following decade. For the first time since the new state was founded there was now a real possibility of work at home in Ireland, and of advancement in various professions. Free secondary education gave people a chance to acquire knowledge and skills. More importantly, it gave opportunities to grow in confidence. People from the rural parts of Ireland, who grew up in what would now be regarded as poverty and deprivation, had the possibility of attending universities. How many of my generation, and those immediately before me, entered seminaries because they saw little other opportunity of a fulfilled life, of pursuing a career? Many of those choices were made at a subconscious level in a society that attached status and security to priesthood. When things began to open up in the secular world the option for priesthood was re-evaluated and, in the words of Monica Baldwin, 'a leap over the wall' was a less daunting prospect.

The new thinking of the Second Vatican Council stressed the importance of lay people and their vital role in the Church in the transmission of the faith. It was now seen that holiness and the duty of spreading the gospel was not solely the domain of the ordained cleric – it was part and parcel of the life of every baptised person. If this was so, why would young men deprive themselves of the intimacy of marriage? They could strive for personal holiness, and they could serve people without becoming priests. By the late 1960s, the traditional stigma of the 'spoiled priest' had begun to disappear. Looking back now I can see that all the signs were emerging that would result in the empty seminaries and the ageing priesthood that is a dramatic feature of the Church today.

While seminarians were leaving in great numbers and the average lay person was becoming more educated, the people in authority in the Irish Church were not tuned in to the Second Vatican Council, were not reading the signs of the times. Bishops John Charles McQuaid of Dublin, Cornelius Lucey of Cork and Michael Browne of Galway, the three dominant clerical voices at the time, were so much part of the old, stagnant clerical Church that they were incapable of imagining that a day would come when it would all fall apart. The gospel saying, 'I will be with you always, to the end of time', was regularly trotted out. Among those in authority in the Church there seemed to be no doubt that the Church as it existed then was exactly as Jesus intended it to be, and that he would ensure that it continued to the end of the world. That gave a degree of certainty, of total assurance, that made it almost impossible for the authorities of the time to be open to new ideas and new ways of expressing the faith. It was a dismal failure of Church leaders and thinkers that they identified the systems and structures of the Church of their day with Christ, and that this excused them from asking any serious questions. They were adamant that the Church as it existed was exactly what Jesus Christ had planned. Furthermore, that same Church had an infallible leader, the pope, who, because of his direct line to God, would not, under any circumstances, lead the Church astray. It just couldn't go wrong. A lot has been written about Archbishop McQuaid, but in many ways Bishop Browne of Galway was a more domineering and arrogant character, though less of a public figure. In his posture and attitude he displayed many of the characteristics of a medieval lord. Bishop Lucey of Cork was a different sort of person. He espoused and preached a strong message of social justice at a time when it wasn't a noticeable feature of Church teaching here in Ireland. He was noted for sermons that contained a critique of the state of the country, or the plight of the small farmers or the rural shopkeepers, or other social justice issues, particularly as they affected rural areas, at confirmation ceremonies. At least that is what was released to the newspapers of the time, whether or not he actually delivered those talks at the ceremony. If he did, I don't know what the young people receiving the sacrament made of them. But he was of the generation who believed you should speak to the adults present, rather than try to communicate with the children. Bishop Lucey had the ability to connect with ordinary people. My father loved him without ever having met him, and eagerly read the accounts of his sermons in the daily paper. However, while he was more in tune with the day-to-day issues of his flock and had a good understanding of social problems, like the rest of his colleagues he was unable to grasp problems developing in the Church, or the central message of the Second Vatican Council – that the Church was the people of God, the community of believers.

Paradoxically, while the Second Vatican Council was meant to revive the Catholic Church, it carried within it the seeds of the Church's decline. While at one level it injected life and energy into the Church, it also introduced new and potentially disturbing ideas: the concept of freedom of conscience, religious liberty and ecumenism. These ideas encouraged people to think for themselves, and the Church structures were not suited to coping with primacy of conscience and freedom of thought. This was really a case of trying to put new wine into old wineskins. The attempt to sew the new patch of personal autonomy into the old garment of obedience and conformity failed. Church authorities sought to keep their options open, to keep a foot in both camps; yes, there was freedom of conscience, but this conscience must be formed by Church teaching. This was the catch-22. Had they been open to the idea that the Church that had emerged in the sixteenth century, after the Reformation and the Council of Trent, was not the only model, things might have been different. There are some indications that the early centuries of the Church had a degree of freedom, but the second millennium was noted for suppression – suppression of thought, of expression and of action. Obedience was the dominant virtue: obedience to the dictates of Church authorities, particularly to what was known as the magisterium, the teaching authority of the Vatican. It is ironic that the Church, whose only *raison d'être* was to propagate the message of Jesus of Nazareth, the person who said that he had come to set people free, had developed an aversion, indeed a fear, of personal freedom of any sort. Over the centuries of the second millennium the Church did everything it could to prevent people from thinking or acting for themselves, and its big weapon of control was the threat of eternal damnation. The message of hell and damnation got people to do largely what they were told, and distrust their own judgement. Bob Dylan's lyrics expressed the era that we lived through very well: 'the times they are a-changin'.' Freedom was in the air. Seminarians who wanted to choose marriage, priests who were honest enough to acknowledge that celibacy was too high a price for priesthood, made their personal decisions, no longer in fear of the Church. This could have been an opportunity to hand over the running of parishes to lay people, but that did not happen because most priests still held on to their control, and the people were not sufficiently educated in the faith to take on the challenge. Throughout the following decades there was no real acknowledgement of or preparation for the decline in vocations to a priesthood that demanded celibacy. Little attention was paid to the fact that many younger people had stopped attending Mass, and by the 1980s and 90s other issues had caught the attention of the laity, and the rot had firmly set in.

Why did I stay during all those years when so many others left, some of them very close friends, including my own brother? I don't know the answer. I know that on one or two occasions during those ten years I was close to leaving, but for whatever reason I hung in there. These were still the heady days after the Second Vatican Council, and, despite the exodus from seminaries and convents, we still believed that there were bright days ahead for the Church.

My book on religious life, published 23 years ago, was not well received in the official structures of the Church. I had written it after spending six years as superior of the largest and oldest Redemptorist monastery in Ireland, Mount St Alphonsus in Limerick, and I was making the case that religious life as we had known it for the previous 200 years was in terminal decline. Many of my colleagues labelled this view as 'too pessimistic', but I saw things differently. The position of rector of the monastery gave me a first-hand view of the actual situation. Very few young men were showing any interest in joining our communities any more, and, among those who did enlist, the commitment appeared to be conditional, temporary. I recall one of them stating that he would give priesthood ten years and then review his options. This man was sincere, talented and well-balanced. This was very typical of the life view of many of these younger men. I accompanied a number of them who made their exit during those years, and they often cited celibacy as the stumbling block to remaining in the priesthood. They believed in God, they enjoyed the work, but they were not prepared to live without a sexual companion. They were aware of the price of foregoing human intimacy and believed that the cost would be damaging to their humanity. So I wrote out of the experience of that time, but few, if any, in key positions in the Church agreed with me, rather they dismissed my views as doom and gloom. The inability of Church institutions to face up to the reality of what was happening under their noses was striking, and instead they convinced themselves that everything would work out grand and that life would continue largely as it had in the past. In fact, the sad reality of both male and female religious life in convents and monasteries today is considerably worse that I had imagined when I wrote that book. I know it is difficult for any institution to accept its own impending demise, but we members of the Church are supposed to be different. We are meant to see our institutions merely as vehicles in the service of a greater end; a greater degree of detachment should have marked us. My experience is the opposite; like Dylan Thomas, we are not able to 'go gentle into that good night'. As I write this I have recently attended a chapter meeting of the Irish Redemptorist province where a lot of time was spent talking about amalgamating with other European units, who, like ourselves, are no longer sufficiently viable to retain their independence.

The revelation of clerical child abuse is often cited as the reason for the decline of the Catholic Church in Ireland, but the roots of the collapse go back much further. The type of Church that developed in the second half of the nineteenth century, probably even the Church that came out of the Council of Trent a few hundred years earlier, contained within itself, I believe, the seeds of its own downfall. It turned its back on the ancient Celtic beliefs and practices, and instead became dominated by Roman ways, Roman structures and Roman thinking. Religious orders like my own, the Redemptorists, introduced continental styles of religious practice, with an emphasis on regular church attendance, frequent confession and devotional forms of prayer. A particular focus was placed on moral behaviour, with special concentration on sexuality and relationships. It could be said that the prominence given to the sixth and ninth commandments (the ones to do with sex and relationships) robbed people of joy in life and of normality in sexual development, and generated anxiety and fear, both at a personal level and within marriage. Religious belief and practice lost the Celtic sense of ease and freedom, and was replaced by a narrow moralistic preaching and practice, focusing on mortal sin and hell. This gradually turned Irish Catholicism into something burdensome and fearful, leaving people apprehensive and afraid – afraid of God and afraid of eternal damnation. Scrupulosity became an all too common feature of people's religious living, driving them constantly into confession boxes to recite the same list of sins and worries, desperately enquiring from the priest if God had forgiven them. It was a joyless, pathetic state, which at its worst turned into serious mental disorder.

The other legacy of the Roman style of religion was what is now commonly referred to as clericalism. Our Catholic religion was based on top-down organisation and belief. The pope was worshipped as almost equal to God; he had the title Vicar of Christ, which implied that he was in the place of Christ, and it conferred the mind and wish of Christ on all his utterances. The Cardinal Archbishop of Armagh was his local equivalent, and had to be treated by all with total respect and deference. The Archbishop of Dublin was a more powerful person than any political leader. This clerical power and authority went all the way down to the parish priest, who was seen as the most authoritative Catholic in the parish. Of course people can hold power only if others cede it to them, and the clerical figures were dominant because many people were convinced that they were somehow holier than the rest of the populace. Many of these men were decent human beings, but while the laity was trapped in the idea that the clergy were more trustworthy and morally superior to the common man and woman, the clergy themselves were equally ensnared by the roles they occupied. The parish priest was expected to have the final say in anything to do with the

Church, and while that might have been somewhat tolerable, a bigger problem was that his 'final say' extended to the other areas in life. He became the chairman of the sports organisations, the local drama society, and whatever else was happening in the parish. The clerical dominance of life generated considerable bitterness among the artistic community due to the Church-inspired censorship of books, films and other expressions of creativity. There were well-known examples, books such as *The Tailor and Ansty*, films such as *The Rose Tattoo*, and writers like John McGahern and Edna O'Brien. The Church had managed to alienate a group of people who were imaginative, spiritually aware and generally not acquisitive or greedy; in other words, people who embodied some of the teachings of our founder, Jesus Christ. There was also a multi-layered resentment among ordinary Catholics, who continued to practise their faith but who carried deep hurt and anger about the arrogance and domineering attitudes of some priests and bishops. I remember when my sister, back in the early 1960s, decided to enter a convent. She chose to go to one in an adjoining diocese, rather than in her own diocese where she had attended secondary boarding school. When she went to her parish priest to get her baptismal certificate, which was necessary for entering a convent, the priest was clearly angry, and questioned her closely as to why she had not chosen to enter a convent in her own diocese. Eventually he gave her the certificate, and as he showed her out the door of the presbytery he sent her off with the words: 'Small loss you'll be, anyway!' A few weeks later, at a station Mass in the village, he challenged our mother as to why she was 'sending' her daughter to a 'foreign' convent. Our mother, who was a tough little woman, gave him her answer in such a way as to finish the conversation. That might seem like a trivial little exchange in today's Ireland, but back in the early 1960s it was anything but trivial. That particular priest ruled the parish – which he was wont to refer to as 'his' parish – with a rod of iron, and to stand up to him could have negative consequences for any family. A word from the parish priest could seriously affect a young person's opportunities in life. That was brought home to me when, a few days before she died almost 40 years later, my mother, on her deathbed, recounted the whole story to me again, and I could see she still carried the hurt of it. This latent anti-clericalism existed side by side with the notion that the cleric was closer to God than the ordinary man or woman in the street.

After the Second Vatican Council, when the Redemptorists were updating their message and method of mission preaching (something that badly needed to be done by the order that had become known as the hellfire preachers), it was decided that, as part of the work in a parish, there would be small group discussions with the missioners in local houses. In this we were following the conciliar teaching about the equality of all the baptised, and that the Church should not only be a preaching Church, but also a listening Church. We encountered a difficulty that we had not anticipated. When people got their voice, they had plenty to say, and very often what came out was generations of hurt and anger towards the Church. This was from the people who were still attending church, the believers. As missioners we were probably not prepared for that, because we too were part of the clerical system and not used to criticism; it wasn't easy for us, or for the local clergy, to hear the institution we represented being decried as domineering and overbearing. It was difficult to deal with, but we knew that no progress would be made until people had their say. We had to listen, even if it did not come easily to us, but I believe it was an important learning point for us. We realised that lay people had to have their voices heard if our missions were to have any impact on parish life. When I recall that period I recognise that it should not have come as a surprise to us that when the cracks began to appear, and the power of the Church, at national and local level, began to wane, many people quickly lost respect for the institution and its leaders.

Many commentators on Church affairs that I have read have suggested that the collapse of the Church in Ireland began with the clerical sex abuse scandal. The seeds were sown much earlier than that, due to the arrogance, born out of excessive power, of many bishops and priests, and the negative, life-denying message that was the normal output from church pulpits at the time. But the first really noticeable crack in the edifice of Church power was the encyclical on artificial birth control, *Humanae Vitae*, in 1968. I think it is generally, though not unanimously, acknowledged that this was a mistaken document by Pope Paul VI. Looking back on it now, specifically from the Irish context, I think that the real damage was done not so much by the document itself, which actually contains some very worthwhile material on human love and relationships, but by the rigid way in which it was imposed on the people by the Irish hierarchy. As usual, the Church authorities did not stress the positive elements of the encyclical, but homed in on the negative, telling people that they could not use contraceptives to limit their family size. Following on from the tradition of Church teaching that every transgression in the area of sexuality was a mortal sin, leading, unless repented, to eternal damnation, there was an insistence that anyone who practised artificial means of contraception was on the road to hell, and that unless they confessed their sin, and stopped using artificial contraception, by their very actions they had broken off all relationship with God. This, coming from a celibate male clergy, caused people to challenge what we men could know about such matters; having answered their own question and decided that it was not exactly our area of expertise, they dismissed the papal letter as irrelevant and, rightly, made their own decisions.

What could the Church have done? Instead of branding actions as mortal sins, and using the threat of hell, they could have recognised this situation as an ideal opportunity to instruct people on the use of individual conscience. They would have needed to move away from the standard Church teaching on conscience, which is that a person could use their conscience, but only if it was informed by the teaching of the Church. They could have helped people to evaluate the particular circumstances of their own lives, weigh them against the teaching of the encyclical, and then have the confidence to make their own personal decisions, which is really what the exercise of individual conscience is all about. Having done that, it would be important that Church authorities, bishops and priests, would fully respect and accept the decisions people made regarding their own lives. But so many priests and bishops were so hung up on the notion of sin that they couldn't accept that the designation of an action as sinful is ultimately between the individual and God, rather than what the Catechism or canon law says. One of the difficulties that Church spokespersons have is the failure to use direct, clear communication. There is always a tendency to hedge bets, to say 'on the one hand, and on the other hand'. This was evident in the response of some of the more 'liberal' clergy to *Humanae Vitae*. Some proposed that using artificial contraception could, in certain circumstances, be the lesser of two evils, and in that sense it could be partially justified, but that the person must continue to go to confession and confess their 'sin'. This was a sort of pathetic effort at keeping in with both sides of the situation. Not only does this approach fail to trust people's own ability to make decisions about their personal lives, it contained another danger. There were many priests hearing confession at the time who were holding to the most rigid position, and a penitent meeting with one of these in the confession box in these circumstances would be likely to be thrown out. This was, sadly, a common feature of the time.

I believe that if the Church had used the opportunity to give proper instruction on forming one's conscience, it would have changed the face of Catholicism, and by now we would have a much more mature and confident Church. If only Pope Francis had been around then, with that great statement from early in his pontificate, in *The Joy of the Gospel*: 'We are called to form consciences, not to replace them.'

In order to assist people in the formation of conscience the Church would have had to be prepared to give up the control it exercised over people's personal lives, a control made possible through dogmatic teaching on sex and relationships, and through the use of the confessional. In hindsight it is obvious that they were not willing to do that, and the result for the Church has been catastrophic. It was deeply ingrained in the system, and in the people who controlled it, that the clerical world (priests, bishops, cardinals and pope) had all the knowledge and all the answers, and what the ordinary people in the pews thought or believed was of no consequence. If the clerics were to start listening to the people and really hearing what they were saying, they would have had to cede their power and control. It must be noted that this clinging to power is not peculiar to the clergy – we see it all the time among other professionals who hold tightly to a body of knowledge related to their particular discipline, be it medicine or law for example, and do not welcome sharing this expertise with their particular laity. It is the very exceptional person with power who is capable of letting go of it willingly. The indications were that there were few of those exceptional people inhabiting the clerical world at the time of *Humanae Vitae*. I once heard a female theologian state that it was a defining moment for the Church – a moment when it might have taken a different direction, a direction that might have, as Robert Frost said, 'made all the difference'. All of this coincided with the introduction of free secondary education and the growth of the universities. People were now being educated like never before, and had both the knowledge and the confidence to think for themselves. When they concluded that one particular aspect of Catholic moral teaching didn't make sense to them, they began to question many more teachings. It was remarkable how quickly the edifice began to cave in once the first stone was removed.

From then on it was downhill for the Catholic Church in Ireland. For me the most amazing feature of the Irish Catholic Church in the past 40 years is the utter failure of anybody in leadership to acknowledge what was happening in front of our eyes, and to make some effort to deal with it. There were efforts at adult education and many lay people availed of the opportunity to learn more about their faith as mature adults. However, when these people attempted to implement any changes within their parish they usually came up against a clerical stone wall. In cases where the priest was open to such lay involvement the implemented changes could come to a quick end when that priest was moved on to another parish. In fairness it must also be said that not all the laity were of one mind, and there was often resentment towards the people who had taken the trouble to study theology, so that the priest was likely to be caught in the middle. For the most part Church leaders just carried on as their ancestors had before them, seemingly convinced that the evidence of dramatic change happening all around them was only an illusion, and that really things would continue as before, as long as they continued to administer the systems and structures they had inherited. An example is their response to the rapid decline in the number of priests, and the high average age of those who are still with us. The fall-off in numbers entering seminaries was obvious since the late 1960s, and a shortage of priests was bound to be a consequence of this. Could it be possible that the authorities did not recognise what was happening? One bishop recently admitted that it took him by surprise, when he belatedly saw that he was running short of priests to staff his parishes. I know that bishops can sometimes live in a bit of a bubble, but is it possible anyone could be that out of touch? I suspect not. I think that they could see what was happening, but that the implications of it were overwhelming, and it was easier to say their prayers and hope that with God's help things would turn around. Praying for vocations did not make much sense when it was blindingly obvious that the old system of male clerical priesthood was no longer credible and that all the prayers in the world wouldn't change that. I think of the line from Dylan Thomas: 'Rage, rage, against the dying of the light'.

Why didn't some of those men, who believed so deeply in the traditional form of church, show some rage against its dying? Why didn't they rise up and go out to fight the battle against the modern world that they so abhorred? Where was their energy, their leadership? I believe a couple of factors were at work. The type of men chosen for episcopal office for the past 40 years or so would have been incapable of leading a credible struggle against secular consumerism. They were chosen because of their orthodoxy, and for the fact that they hadn't ever put their heads up to question the Church on any issue. In other words, our episcopal palaces were mostly occupied by submissive, timid men who kept their heads down. I also suspect that some of them didn't really believe very much in what they preached, but stayed with it for the sake of the honour and distinction of their position. Maybe that is a harsh judgement, but I have noted the change in tone of some of them when they eventually retired. Only then did they feel free to raise issues like the rule on compulsory celibacy. There was one notable exception, Bishop Willie Walsh of Killaloe.

Whatever the reason for the silence of the hierarchy, the sad fact is that the Catholic Church in Ireland is fading away, not with a raging struggle, not with a bang, but with little more than a whimper. Sad indeed, because many a baby is being thrown out with this particular bathwater, and some of the voices that proclaim the great modern Ireland, freed from the bondage of the Church, have little enough to offer in its place.

2

The Divine Mystery: Who, What, Where Is God?

Diarmuid Ó Murchú addresses his 2017 book, *Incarnation*, to a group he calls the wise elders. He defines these 'wise elders' as mature adults of 60-plus who are intellectually curious. They are willing to explore their spirituality, are often uneasy with the dogmas of formal religion, and are seeking a forum where their exploration of faith can become the subject of serious and reflective dialogue. He goes on to say that many of these 'wise elders' will still be churchgoers but tend not to look to a formal church or religion for the serious and fruitful deepening of their faith. Australian writer Kevin Treston and Czech theologian Tomas Halik, writing in a similar vein, refer to them as 'seekers'.

I don't know about the 'wise' part, but I see myself as a seeker, and I find myself increasingly uneasy with the proliferation of dogma in formal religion. This is a somewhat unsettling, but also extremely interesting, place to be as I proceed through the eighth decade of my existence on this planet, because as the years move on I am finding new meaning, a new way of looking at and language to express my understanding of myself, life and religious belief. This development in my life has been greatly influenced by my brush with the Vatican. The consequences of that, meaning eight years of suspension from priestly ministry, have caused me to move inexorably away from the influence of religious life and formal Church structures and given me the freedom to think differently about religious dogma without the fear that I might be losing my faith. I can now see that during all those years when I lived in monasteries and preached sermons in various churches around the country, I did not fully comprehend the extent to which my thinking, and even my exposure to ideas and attitudes, was to a fair degree curtailed and limited – restricted as much by myself, my inner self, as by the circumstances of my life and work. My preaching was mostly done in the context of parish missions and novenas, religious events aimed at the renewal and deepening of the faith of the listeners, so I could not allow myself seriously to question some of what were seen as doctrines that were basic to the faith. I suppose I followed the diktat of Goethe, who said something like 'Give me your certainties; I have enough doubts of my own'. Looking back, I feel certain discomfiture at the notion that my preaching, or anybody else's, could deepen the faith of another person. That is the job of each individual as they follow the guidance of the Spirit. If truth be told, there were times when I preached as certainties things about which I had many questions and doubts. Is that what institutions do to us? To be fair to myself and to others who preach, the most we can do is provide a modicum of influence in people's lives. I am aware that there were also times when I pushed the boat out a little in my preaching, even on occasion flirting with what some would regard as heresy, and in the end I suppose that caught up with me, leaving me in the position I now find myself in relation to the official Church.

So, what dogmas am I now finding it difficult to accept as I move on in my human and spiritual journey? At Sunday Mass we recite the Nicene Creed:

I believe in God, the Father Almighty,
creator of heaven and earth;
I believe in Jesus Christ, his only son Our Lord,
born of the Father before time began;
God from God, light from light, true God from true God,
begotten not made, consubstantial with the Father ...

These sentences have their origin in the fourth century, at the Council of Nicaea in 325. This council was called by the Emperor Constantine, who, for his own political purposes, had allowed the Christian religion to be freely practised in the Roman Empire. There were at the time serious disputes going on among the believers in the newly burgeoning Church about the nature of God, and who exactly Jesus was, and the purpose of this council was to clear up these matters for all time. The problem here is with the notion of 'for all time'. We do not live in a static universe; rather it is a dynamic, constantly changing world that is being created anew in every generation. The council produced the Nicene Creed, with its description of God as a being resident in heaven, made up of three persons: Father, Son and Holy Ghost (or Spirit, as we now refer to the third person). It goes on to tell us that the Son is 'consubstantial with the Father'. All of this has to be an extraordinarily detailed statement about the nature of the divine coming from human beings. But the really damaging part was that the council went on to declare all of these statements to be dogmas of faith that had to be accepted and believed in their literal meaning by Church people till the end of time, and it branded as heretics those who did not accept them. It is somewhat understandable that those who drew up these statements about God were seeking to give clarity and direction to believers and, like many human groups, were trying to impose unity – which can be a rather futile exercise. The real tragedy was, and is, the unwillingness of future generations of Church councils to look again at these dogmas and to realise that they were time-limited, that they belonged to the fourth century and they now present the modern Church with a major problem that will not be easily solved.

John Feehan accurately pinpoints the nature and extent of the problem in an article in the book *Responding to* Laudato Si': he notes that this definition of God was formulated to quell what he calls the 'speculative theological turmoil' that was rife in the early fourth century and goes on to say that these dogmas of the Nicene Creed are steeped in 'a child's grasp of what creation means'. Feehan, quoting Charles Raven, a Church of England minister who lived in the early part of the last century, points out that, as limited human beings we can speak with any degree of certainty only about things that we experience and so have to beware of claiming to have full knowledge of the nature of God.

These views of Feehan and Raven sum up the difficulty I have when I am asked to join the priest in reciting the Creed at Mass. It is a bit like asking me, in my 70s, to express my faith in the prayers that I learned as a small child. They were perfectly adequate and good for me at that stage, but now I need something more in tune with the stage of life and understanding I have reached.

Herein lies the problem. As time advances, and as our knowledge and understanding of creation and the universe increase, we are led more and more into the extraordinary mystery of everything. Precise definitions from many centuries ago are now being seen as completely inadequate, and insufficient, by many believers. Unfortunately the teaching Church has the very false and damaging principle that it cannot contradict or correct any statement of a previous council or pope, because the Church/pope is seen as the voice of God – remember the term 'Vicar of Christ' – and how then could it possibly be that God would change his mind? That's the theory. In practice the Church has often changed its teaching down through history, but it still likes to claim that it is unchanging. So we are stuck with a definition of God based on an understanding of creation and humanity from almost 2,000 years ago, and expressed in the language of that age; furthermore, it is demanded, under pain of serious sin, that we give assent to this definition. Let me give some illustrations of what I mean.

We were told that he (always a 'he'!) created the universe in six days some four or five thousand years ago, which people in the fourth century believed was the length of time since the world was created. Our knowledge of the universe and how it all began and how it continues in existence has evolved and continues to evolve. This knowledge gives us a dramatically different perspective from which to view our faith in a divine presence, in God.

The best estimate we have now is that the universe is in existence for something like 13.7 billion years – a far cry from the few thousand years that the people in the fourth century believed. We also now know that the creation of the universe, far from being a historical event that began and ended at a certain time in the past, is a current and continuing reality. Kevin Treston, in his book *Who Do You Say I Am?*, puts it this way: 'The world, and indeed the whole of the universe, is always in a state of becoming, always creating.'

The universe is constantly expanding and developing, and our earth, which was believed by the people who defined the nature of God so many centuries ago, to be flat, and to be the centre of the universe, we now know to be round, to be one of a number of planets travelling around the sun, in our particular galaxy, which is only one of many thousands or millions of galaxies. In other words the earth, our world as we know it, is just a tiny little dot in this wonderful, constantly expanding universe. We were also led to believe that this three-person God dwelt in a place in the sky or, in a place above us, called heaven, and the gospels give us the picture of Jesus ascending from this earth to the heavenly home when he had finished his work here on earth. In this heavenly dwelling God the Father is reputed to be sitting on his throne, with Jesus at his right hand, distant from, but guiding and controlling all that happens here. More worryingly, this God on the throne was depicted as standing in judgement on all of humanity.

All of this stretches credibility to its limits for Diarmuid Ó Murchú's wise elders or Kevin Treston's seekers, who have come to some appreciation of the extraordinary mystery of our universe, and who have learned to ponder in awe and wonder the beauty and complexity of creation. Some scientists are even learning to stand back in wonder when they discover the countless millions of tiny cells, working together in harmony, that keep each individual human being in existence; and not just humans, but all of creation, from the tiniest creatures and plants to the immensity of space. Even the least complex of plants, the magnolia flower, for example, or the tiniest of creatures, all share the same complex structure of interacting cells that make up our own bodies. The more I read about this, and ponder on it, the more I am faced with the mystery of it all, the mystique of each one of us, the more I am faced with not how much I know but how little I know. How or what or who is keeping this entire universe in harmony? Does it all happen by accident or chance, as some scientists believe? Maybe it does, but the more I learn about it, the more I find it impossible to accept that chance is at the heart of it. It might be because I have believed in a God all my life, but I find it impossible to accept that there is not some guiding hand, some great consciousness, maybe a collective consciousness, embedded in it all, delighting in the works of its hand.

So where do I stand now on the idea of God? Is there such a presence, and, if so, what can we now say about it? Yes, I do believe in a divine reality – I am unable to allow that God is just a social construct that we have created to meet our personal needs – but I know that this divinity is shrouded in mystery, and the best anyone can do is get glimpses of the presence, and to experience touches of love in the course of our lives. We have to go back to the writings of St John, who tells us that

God is love: 'Wherever there is love, there is God'. Trying to define this mystery, to describe it, to say where it can be found and what exactly is its nature, is foolish, futile and damaging. It is harmful because it kills the mystery, and that is why I cannot say the Creed with any conviction any more. The only way I can cope with it is to take it as figurative imagery from long ago, when people, using the knowledge and understanding they had at the time, tried to say something that might help them explore the mystery. At that level I can join in, knowing that today, with our knowledge and experience, we would use different imagery and language as we try to grasp what still is, and will continue to be, beyond our understanding. Certain words from the Creed resonate with me – creation, light, truth – these images speak a positive message about the Spirit of the Divine.

Apart from what resonates with me, what do I believe? For a start, I no longer believe this presence is a male figure resident somewhere in the sky, which we call heaven, and who is willing to intervene in the ins and outs of our lives. The complexity of creation, both in its expanse and it its minutiae, is extraordinary. The more we learn, the more questions we have, and the more we wonder at it all. I am convinced now by those who say that all of this does not happen by chance, just as my own life did not come about by chance. I believe there is an ultimate purpose at work in creation. There is some guiding hand, some energy that keeps it all in existence, and it is in creation that I now seek to find God – in people, in the material universe, in the circumstances and vicissitudes of life. At this stage of my life, the life that I believe was given to me by a God who is the source of every breath that I breathe, I tend to think and speak of God as divine presence, divine energy, or maybe ultimate purpose. This is at the centre and core of what I am suggesting in this book. It cannot of course be proven; it is buried in the depth of mystery, and so this is where faith comes in. I choose to believe, and it makes great sense to me now, that there is a divine presence at the centre and heart of everything, including each one of us and everything around us. Pope Francis says the following in the great document on the environment that he wrote a few years ago, *Laudato Si'*: 'God's divine presence continues the work of creation. The universe unfolds in God, who fills it completely. Faith allows us to interpret the meaning and the mysterious beauty of what is unfolding.'

So I am more inclined to look for God, divine reality, in the world around me, in people, in nature, and in the circumstances of our lives. I am less inclined to do my searching for the divine presence in a physical church, or before a tabernacle. It is not that I believe it is not there, and I have total respect for those who find God there, but for me the Divine is more readily experienced in the expanse, in the wonder and in the mystery. I believe that all of life is shot, inoculated, with the divine presence of a loving God.

There are a great number of people writing about this, especially in recent years, and they all have one basic idea in common. They reject the notion of a distant God, up in a heavenly realm. John Feehan, in his book *God in a Five-Pointed Star*, writes about where the Divine is present for him and states clearly that when we encounter beauty in any way, we are not experiencing a reflection of God, we are actually experiencing the life of the living God. Feehan uses lyrical language in describing such an encounter with beauty: 'We are in the presence of God. I am with God. I am in God. And God is in me, as he is in the buttercup or the butterfly or the spider ... Creation is the garden God walks in and we are invited to walk with him.' For Feehan, all creatures, great and small, are an expression of the creator and something of God materialises in them.

In this we are getting in touch with a very different notion of God from the one that we learned in our early religious education. This divine presence is not a distant figure, up in a heavenly dwelling away from us and our lives, but is instead at the heart of each one of us and of all of creation, and is constantly active, calling us to the fulfilment of the ultimate purpose, which is perfect love. This is no longer a God that can be explained and described, as the Nicene Creed claims to do. Instead it is mystery, beyond our comprehension, but something we can come to experience to the limited extent of which we are capable in our human condition. In this faith-filled way of looking at the universe we are able to see evolution as the work of the divine creator, gradually achieving the ultimate purpose, which is the coming together of all of creation in the experience of perfect love. This is what Teilhard de Chardin called the Omega Point. For me, the main message is that the world is good, that it is constantly being recreated by God and that God works through us in this work of ongoing creation. God's love accompanies us all through our lives; we haven't done anything to gain it or to earn it; it is freely given. We can only co-create the world with God if we live in love, which means respecting and caring for the entire universe.

I grew up with the idea of a static, unchanging God. I now believe that there is a divine presence of love and energy underlying and infusing the universe and our lives, but I believe that this divine presence is constantly evolving, growing and changing because the universe is always evolving. To some extent, as Catholics we are still a bit nervous of the concept of evolution, but as Diarmaid Ó Murchú claims, in his book *Incarnation*, the notion of evolution has 'entered even religious discourse ... people are no longer drawn to a religion of fixity and rigid doctrinal truths'. I can now recognise that this idea of an evolving God is not that new. I recall the 1970s and talking to someone who had attended a theology course at a Catholic university in California who was discussing the concept of 'God in process'. To be truthful, I did not really grasp the meaning of this. I still don't claim to understand it fully, but it makes more sense to me than the notion of a fixed deity observing the universe from afar.

I am well aware that this is an enormous change in my way of thinking about faith and religious belief. For me it is a journey that I don't think I could have been on but for the fact that I had been forbidden to minister as a priest. As I have said earlier, this event in my life has given me the freedom to think in new ways and to explore new understandings. It is both an unsettling and an exciting thing to be doing in the latter years of my life on this earth. But I am glad to leave behind me something that Ó Murchú describes well when he says, 'All the major religions advocate childlike dependence, which all too often morphs into childish subservience.'

Childish subservience is, in my opinion, an accurate enough description of a lot of our traditional attitudes towards our faith, and this subservience exonerated us from taking personal responsibility for our lives. We went along blindly with whatever the Church taught, therefore we did not have to go to the trouble of exercising our own critical faculties. But that is no longer the case, either for the 'wise elders', the seekers, or, even more so, for the generations of the future. Some people might interpret the fact that we are questioning ancient doctrines as a sign that we are losing the faith. I don't believe this to be the case. Rather we are searching for new language, new understandings, even new metaphors that will help us get in touch with the divine mystery. When we do that, the mysterious Spirit that we now begin to perceive is far more immense and more attractive than the heavenly God in the sky we were taught about in the past. The mistake that was made by the teachers of the faith in the past was to believe that they could define and describe, once and for all time, the ultimate mystery. It was both arrogant and foolish of them and of the Church in times past when they proclaimed these beliefs as defined dogmas to be accepted by believers for all the ages. They failed to recognise the enormous depth of the mystery that was all around them, and they wanted to tame it by describing and defining it. In other words, they wanted to reduce the divine creator to a manageable god that human minds could understand. When we, as mere humans, try to define mystery we do not come to the truth, rather we block others from coming to an awareness of the depth and richness of the mystery. Definition and dogma kill mystery. The religious journey that many of us are now on is not to understand the mystery, but to try to link in to it in whatever way we can, to be open to the wonder of it all, and to realise that we too are part of that mystery, that wonder. So, for instance, we look anew at the traditional teaching about God being a Trinity of Three Persons, Father, Son and Holy Spirit. It is not a description, a definition, of God. That is impossible for us. The idea of the Divine Trinity, three manifestations of the one mysterious unity, is a beautiful image, an image of unity, of cooperation, of community, of ultimate love. It opens up for us important aspects of the nature of the Divine, but it does not describe or define God. It is a very useful metaphor, and we humans must be realistic and humble enough to know that when it comes to understanding or describing the great mysteries of life and the universe, and most of all the Divine, the best we can do, and ultimately all we need to do, is use image and metaphor. For that reason I would suggest again that it might be helpful for us to limit our use of the word 'God', because it conjures up images of the male figure in the heavenly realm – an image of divinity that came from a time when the world was ruled by kings and princes, who lived in lavish palaces and ruled over their subjects. We seem to have gotten things upside down and backwards. Instead of God creating humans in his image and likeness, as the Book of Genesis says, we humans created God in our image and likeness – the male, patriarchal lord and king abiding in the heavenly realm, remote from the lives of people. This is part of the core dogma of our faith, which constitutes a problem for thinking believers today. Around that image was built a whole spirituality with prayer focused on appeasing this distant king, so that he might look kindly on us his subjects.

I am now more comfortable with the notion of a divine presence at the heart of creation, a divine presence within each one of us, a divine presence that is continuously creating and who involves us as essential partners in this ongoing act of creation. This divine presence is not distant, far away, in a heavenly realm, but is part of us, and is keeping everything in existence with an almighty and enduring love. This is not the pantheism of old, it is not suggesting that everything is divine, but rather that every aspect of creation is infused with the Divine Spirit. We don't need to persuade or appease this divinity any more, but just to be aware as best we can of the loving presence in the heart of everything, and to rest in the assurance and security of that presence. So our prayer gradually takes on a different style and content. A friend of mine, in discussing this concept of God as divine mystery, suggested that it poses difficulty for people who find comfort in praying to a personal God. Maybe it is possible for us to rethink the very nature of prayer.

If God is not someone who dispenses favours, where, when and how do we pray? I have a certain trepidation in writing about prayer lest it gives the impression that I do a lot of praying or that I am putting myself in a position where I am telling others how to pray. I think that the answer to my question is that we pray as we can. The question of prayer cannot be considered apart from the absolute belief that God is love and we are loved by God, individually and collectively. It is important to know that the urge to pray, the act of prayer, does not spring from ourselves, it springs from the Spirit of God who lives in our hearts, who sustains our every breath. Spending time in prayer is a way of being open to God's love within us, of recognising our dependence on the Divine, and it enables us to come to terms with the reality that we are not in control of our world. In some ways, the recent pandemic taught us this lesson.

It is my belief that the gift of life is given to us by a loving God and that we come into this world in a state of purest innocence. As we go forward in this life, the sin of humanity, the flawed human condition, the fractured nature of our world contaminate us so that we want to possess, to control, to be important, to be at the centre of all that goes on. Taking time for prayer is a means of moving away from this egotism. We do not pray so as to feel good about ourselves. The old catechism had a definition that is worthy of our attention. It defines prayer as 'a raising up of the heart and mind to God'. If we take out the words 'raising up' in acknowledging that God is not 'up in heaven', we get the idea of prayer as a way of focusing our attention on God. We pray so as to be still in the presence of God who dwells in our hearts. That is the main thing that I have to say about prayer, that it is a time of stillness to which God calls each one of us, a time to just be in the presence of the Divine. Each one of us is called to this and our response to this call demands a certain degree of commitment. If we take this seriously, it should change the way we see ourselves and how we view others. If God dwells in my heart, I must recognise that every other person is also imbued with the Spirit of God. This should keep us from judging others, but many of us struggle in this area.

What about vocal prayer, what about the Rosary, what about the novenas? These are all valid forms of prayer as long as our intentions are right, as long as our hearts are set on the kingdom of God. Of course, our efforts at prayer can often be a struggle and are criss-crossed with multiple distractions. What matters is that we recognise that the call to prayer comes to us from God, not the other way around, and that we don't use prayer as a means of manipulating God. The words of the Our Father, 'thy will be done', sums it up.

We pray much more than we realise. Every time I wish another person well, every time I rejoice in another's good fortune, I am praying. Any time that I am grateful for something, I am praying. We can pray for other people, always in the spirit of acceptance of any possible outcome, and prayer for others is a way of unleashing some type of positive energy in their direction. We do not tell God what to do and it is important to remember the words of Matthew's Gospel – 'The Father knows what you need before you ask him'. We can pray for those who have died, trusting that they are in the eternal life of God, believing that they are gone ahead of us, confident that where they are, we too shall be. We are all one in Christ.

Prayer is the conviction that God is in charge. As is often the case, the poets grasp this and express it better than many of us who seek to discuss prayer. In *Hamlet*, Shakespeare tells us 'There is a Divinity that shapes our ends, Rough hew them how we will'. Hopkins repeats this sentiment when he tells us why 'nature is never spent'. It is because 'the Holy Ghost over the bent / world broods, with warm breast and with, / ah, bright wings'. We can find comfort in the mantra of Julian of Norwich, 'All shall be well, and all shall be well, and all manner of things shall be well'.

In considering the mystery of God and our relationship with this mystery, it is necessary to deal with the Church doctrine on original sin, which does not sit easily with the image of the Divine as the underlying source of creation. The teaching on original sin is problematic from a number of points of view. It is based on the story in the Book of Genesis, the first book of the Bible, where we are told that our first parents, Adam and Eve, sinned in the Garden of Eden, by eating the forbidden fruit, an apple, no less. This bible story tells us that God was so angry with Adam and Eve that he drove them out of the garden, and in his anger closed the gate of heaven to all humankind. God turned his face away and shut humans out. It is important to state here that this story is not historical truth, even if the Catechism of the Catholic Church treats it as if it is; it is an imaginative narrative that seeks to give us an image of our world, of the human condition. It is a metaphor for the fact that we are not always able to live up to ideals; we fail and we are imperfect. What about the notion of an angry, distant God, sitting on his throne in heaven, banishing our first parents? Again, this is metaphorical language, but it fit very well with the medieval world, where kings on thrones regularly got angry, and set out to punish the people or person who offended them by declaring war. By taking a literal interpretation of this story in Genesis, a doctrine of original sin was formulated – that Adam and Eve sinned, that this sin was inherited by every human being after them, and that, along with inheriting the sin, we also inherited the punishment. The gates of heaven were closed against humanity. The acceptance of this teaching is linked with the fact that people believed that creation was a historical event that had happened just a couple of thousand years previously. Now we believe that creation is not just historical. It is also ongoing. It is a continuous reality. We know that the origins of the universe go back over thirteen million years, with humans inhabiting the earth for at least 150,000 years, and possibly a lot longer. Looked at from this perspective, this dogma becomes unacceptable, because it says that the creator God, having created humanity to be companions in eternity, immediately shut them out of heaven for all these thousands of years. The destination of the millions and billions of people who lived between the time that human life appeared on earth and Jesus Christ's death (the event that supposedly opened heaven's gates) has never been explored. No clear explanation was ever given as to where all these millions and billions of people who lived through those years went after death. We are, however, told they did not go to God. The image of God that is projected in this teaching is that of someone who is unloving and uncaring.

The doctrine goes on to say that it took the suffering and death of his only son, Jesus, to appease the anger of God, and reopen the gates of heaven to humanity. God's anger could only be appeased by someone equal to him; this is why it had to be his son who suffered and died on behalf of humanity, and since the act of reparation was performed by God's son, God could now let go of his anger because proper reparation had been achieved by Jesus. This is why Jesus is commonly referred to in Christian theology as the saviour of the world. This adds even more to the image of God as a cruel tyrant, as someone who is angry, vindictive and unforgiving, who nursed his grievance, and would only let go of it when his son endured a horrible death. Forgiveness could be granted only when total reparation was made. This depiction of God is in sharp contrast to the regular descriptions of God in the Old Testament, and especially in the Psalms, where he is addressed as someone who is full of mercy, compassion and forgiveness. 'The Lord is a God merciful and gracious, slow to anger, and abounding in steadfast love and faithfulness'(Exodus 34). The Book of Isaiah gives a rich image of a loving God: 'Can a mother forget the child of her womb ... even should she forget, I will never forget you.'

We are told about how God spoke regularly to the prophets, and how he gave the commandments to Moses. It is important to remember that many, if not all, of these stories are mythological, but they show the belief of the people at the time that God was close to them. There is no indication in the gospels that Jesus understood that God was angry and had closed humanity out. On the contrary, he spoke regularly to the people of his time about the closeness of God to them, even referring to God as 'Father'. For Jesus the Divine was a real and close presence, not only for himself but for every person. Many of his parables, like the one we refer to as the Prodigal Son, give a picture of a God that is totally different from the one portrayed in the teaching around original sin. The image of the Divine as being at the heart of creation is much closer to the type of God that Jesus spoke about than our traditional notion of the heavenly ruler. However, the clear understanding of this is that the gates of eternity were not closed to the people who lived before Jesus, and God's anger did not have to be appeased, because, as the Bible constantly tells us in its metaphorical writings, God's love for humanity, and for the whole of creation, is total and everlasting.

The Divine created, and continues to create, the universe out of love. Diarmuid Ó Murchú stresses that God's love is infinite – outside of time as measured by us. God was loving the world ever before humankind evolved, long before the evolution of the Catholic Church. It is worth quoting Ó Murchú's exact words: 'God has been fully manifesting God's self in the evolutionary unfolding of creation through many eons. Long before humans evolved and long before formal religion or churches ever came to be, God's gracious and empowering creativity inundated every fibre of the cosmic creation.'

In other words, God has been pouring out his enduring and unending love on creation since the very beginning (as humans, we are not able to have any concept of 'the beginning' or 'the end' as we cannot grasp the notion of infinity – something that is outside of time), even long before humans arrived on this earth. This has to be so, because creation is the great act of love by God and that love is certain to endure until the end point (again we must remember that the 'end' is outside of time), what de Chardin called the Omega Point, when love will be the ultimate and the all.

3

What Do We Mean When We Say Jesus Is the Son of God?

*I*n the previous chapter I outlined a new understanding of the universe, creation, our own lives and how we are intimately linked with the whole of creation and imbued by the Spirit of the Divine. This is a substantially different way of looking at things compared to when the early teachers of the Church developed the doctrines that are still at the core of our faith. Based on our notion of God as the basic energy that underlies all of creation and who cannot be limited to time and space, what can we now try to say about Jesus?

It is important to note that during his life Jesus was not known as Jesus Christ. He would probably have been referred to as Jesus of Nazareth; Jesus, son of Joseph and Mary; or maybe 'the carpenter'. The Christ title came later in the writings of Paul and the apostles, and it was a name given to him after his resurrection. Following the raising of Jesus from the dead his followers strongly identified him with the Jewish longing for a saviour, the Messiah. By giving him the name Christ they were asserting that he was the one who had been awaited, the Messiah promised in the Jewish Bible. In John's Gospel, which would have been written at a later date than the letters of Paul, the Christ notion is expanded greatly. He was the Word, who was with God from the beginning, and in fact he was identified as God. What Jesus would have thought about that during his life we do not know. While this type of language is attributed to Jesus, especially in the Gospel of John, it is highly unlikely that he would have used it about himself during his life. Jesus certainly had a close relationship with God, calling God 'Father'. Likewise, he urged each of us to call God 'Father'. John's Gospel, written as we know long after the death of Jesus, and even after John himself had died, was written by the community of believers founded by John. The author or authors had a very specific agenda or purpose in mind: to assert their belief that Jesus was the Christ, and the eternal and unique Son of God. They had gathered around the apostle John, had listened to his stories and teaching about Jesus of Nazareth, and had developed their own faith over the years. Thus the long passages attributed to Jesus in John's Gospel were very unlikely to be his actual words, but rather words put into his mouth by the community to illustrate their understanding of who and what Jesus was and his relationship with God.

What we are getting here is more about the belief around the risen Christ than about the human Jesus. John's Gospel is probably the most difficult to comprehend but, at its core, it also reflects the notion that what we know about God can be summed up in one central concept – God is love. The other three gospels, which we refer to as the synoptic gospels, were also written from their own various perspectives, but they all focused on the belief that Jesus was the one sent by God to be the saviour, the one who was 'to come', the chosen one. In other words, there wasn't from the beginning a common belief about who and what Jesus of Nazareth was. It was only gradually, and due to the writings of Paul and the authors of the four gospels, that some clear and generally accepted notions began to take shape. It cannot be emphasised enough that belief about the person of Jesus did not come down lock, stock and barrel to the early communities of believers, rather it developed grad-ually as an expression of the faith of these communities, an expression of how they made meaning of the life and teachings of Jesus. We also know that up as far as the fourth century there were still very different views and strong debates about the nature of Jesus. What we in the Catholic Church now believe about Jesus of Nazareth was a collection of doctrines that gradually developed over the early centuries of the

Church, rather than something that was accepted and understood by all from the beginning.

Gradually it became the accepted interpretation that Jesus was the exclusive, the only Son of God, and that he was sent by God to redeem a broken world. This was passed on to us as dogma in the Nicene Creed:

We believe in one Lord, Jesus Christ,
the only Son of God,
eternally begotten of the Father.

The fourth-century Council of Nicea was called to put an end to all the debate, and to establish once and for all the truth about Jesus. It is now difficult to question this depiction of Jesus without being considered heretical, but it is important to take a fresh look at who exactly Jesus was, and what the core of his teaching and preaching was. If we take a more contemporary view of the Divinity as the guiding force that underlies our universe, I think it is valid to begin to look in a fresh way at Jesus of Nazareth. To do this comprehensively is well beyond my competence, but I seek to point here to some areas that could repay exploration and analysis.

Jesus did not have to die to save us from our sins, in the traditional understanding of that notion, or to open the gates of heaven to humankind, or to appease the anger of God. There is no indication in the gospels that Jesus saw his life's purpose as having anything to do with that, and he certainly did not believe in an angry God. However, there was a custom in ancient Judaism that might have contributed to this understanding of the role of Jesus. In the Old Testament it was the custom once a year for the high priest to release a goat into the desert, and metaphorically to lay all the sins of the people on the back of the goat. In that sense the goat was the scapegoat, taking away the sins of the people. In the early spiritual writings Jesus of Nazareth came to be seen as the one who took all our sins on his back, like the scapegoat, and reconciled us with God. But it was really only in the writings of St Anselm in the eleventh century that the idea of God insisting that his son must become man, and die a horrible death as an act of appeasement, became established as the accepted way of understanding the purpose of the life and death of Jesus. Our liturgy texts are now littered with this concept. A typical example, taken from Eucharistic Prayer III, is the following: 'Look, we pray, upon the oblation of your Church and, recognising the sacrificial Victim by whose death you willed to reconcile us to yourself ... '.

How can we begin to revisit this doctrine, which doesn't have a basis in the life and teaching of Jesus? If we continue to proclaim as literally true the notion of Jesus having to die to save us from our sins, to reconcile us to the Father, many of our references to God become contradictory. Is he compassionate and loving, or is he unsympathetic, severe and prone to vindictiveness? Is it possible that, having created the human race, God held a grievance against all humanity for thousands, maybe even millions of years? Surely not. Traditional teaching has tended to attempt to justify this with the notion that God is just. But this teaching, that we are all saddled with the sin of our first parents (and again it is important to remember that the description of the fall of Adam and Eve is figurative and not historically true), can hardly be considered just or fair. If God's justice trumps his compassion and mercy, is he, then, a God of love?

Another very damaging effect of this teaching is that it has put the emphasis on the suffering and death of Jesus rather than on his life and message, and this has led to a serious imbalance in the way Jesus is presented in our Church. For instance, the Creed that we recite at Mass, be it the Nicene Creed or the Apostles' Creed, skips from Jesus' birth to his suffering and death. There is no mention of the content of what he preached. His central teaching about what he called the kingdom, or the reign, of God is not mentioned; nothing about his radical inclusiveness, his teaching on justice, reconciliation or discipleship ('Come, follow me'). If these creeds are meant to be statements of Christian belief, they are seriously inadequate. I would ask what is the point of them.

The birth and death of Jesus, like all other elements of creation, are natural and essential parts of the evolutionary process. The manner of Jesus' death, his crucifixion, was a direct result of his life and ministry, and of his radical fidelity to his mission, which presented a challenge to the civil and religious leaders of the time. Jesus was a revolutionary in the best and fullest meaning of that word. The kingdom of God, as he preached it, was a radically different way of living, of relating and of organising society. It is no wonder that the authorities were threatened by him. When we think of Jesus in this way we do not get so absorbed in the minutiae of his crucifixion and death, but instead focus on what was really important about him, his life and message. He came to show us how to live, and the ultimate task of any Christian is to do as those early followers did, to respond to him when he says to us, as he said to them, 'Follow me'. It is by teaching us how to be in this world that Jesus becomes our saviour, because if we live by his teaching we are already becoming part of the Divine life.

This understanding of God as the source and energising force of all life, of all creation, also means that Jesus cannot be seen as the first manifestation, the first revelation, of God in the world. That revelation of God, of the Divine, happened at the beginning of creation, and continues to this day, just as creation is a continuing reality. (We must, of course, always allow for the fact that in speaking of the Divine we are in the realm of something that is outside time and space – there is no beginning, no end.) The Divine Spirit was never absent from creation, indeed could not be, because the Spirit of God was, and continues to be, the heartbeat of all that exists. Creation is the working out of the ultimate purpose of the Divine, who has entrusted us to be partners in this great enterprise. We are constantly creating the world in collaboration with God, as St Paul tells the Philippians – 'God is always at work in you.'

Science tells us that human beings evolved gradually over thousands of years. They are able to describe various stages, like *Homo erectus*, when our ancestors first stood erect and walked on two feet rather than four. All the time the shape of the head developed, with the forehead becoming straighter and the brain area enlarging. Eventually humans developed into what we now call *Homo sapiens*, beings that could think, remember, learn and become creators in their own right. Theologians over the years have wondered when *Homo sapiens* developed a soul, and the usual explanation given is that at a certain point in the evolutionary process God intervened and infused a soul into humanity. This explanation comes from a belief that God is outside, distant, not directly involved in the process of evolution. If we believe, as I am outlining here, that the Divine Spirit is, and was from the beginning, at the heart of creation, then the question of infusing a soul does not arise, because the Divine Spirit has always been there, always present in every human person and in all creation.

So where does that leave Jesus? Who was he? For me that is the wrong question, because I go back again to the notion of the Divine as total mystery, beyond our ability to define or describe. Jesus, in his life and teaching, was the clearest, though not the first, revelation of God to

34

the world. As regards his exact relationship to the mystery he called his Father, and what precisely is meant when we call Jesus the Son of God, I am happy to leave that in the realm of mystery. In whatever way we might understand the resurrection of Jesus, the reality of his powerful presence in the world and in the lives of believers is, I suggest, beyond doubt. His life, his personhood, is manifested in the divine presence at the heart of creation, and I believe that this too is the destiny of each one of us after our physical death. His presence in the world 2,000 years ago was not to assuage the anger of God, but to be for all of us an example of proper living, a model of how to build what he called the kingdom of God in this world. He came to show us the way. And that is why we can do no better than attempt to follow his example in our own lives. For Jesus, this world, and our lives in it, is not the valley of tears that we have to endure in order to attain everlasting happiness in the heavenly realm. He wanted the people of his time to learn that the fundamental purpose of their lives on earth was to be co-workers with the Divine Spirit in creating the kingdom of God in the here and now. The same task is what Christians must be about today, assisted and enabled by the living spirit of Jesus. He outlined for us what the qualities of the kingdom are – peace, justice, joy and love. I am now inclined to believe that there is a real and profound continuation between our lives here on earth and the existence that awaits us after we die. I trust that the struggle and the failure will be over, and that we can rest in peace and love and joy. Will we be subsumed into the great Mystery, or will we retain our own individuality? We will have to wait to find that out. I hope that we will be there as individuals, and that we will continue to love those we have loved in this life. Our experience of the giving and receiving of love is the closest we get in this life to the Divine nature, so I strongly believe that the loves we have known here will continue and reach perfection in the fullness of Divinity. Whatever it will be, I expect our entry into eternity to be a blinding revelation, an eye-opener, in the fullest and deepest sense of the words.

I love the final lines of Chekhov's play, *Uncle Vanya*, as adapted by Brian Friel. The family has fractured during the course of the play, and the only ones left on the stage at the end are Vanya and his niece Sonya. Vanya is depressed, lonely and somewhat rudderless. He turns to Sonya, and in a despairing voice asks her what they can do now. Her reply:

What we must do is endure. We must keep on living and keep on working until the end. And when the time comes for us to die, we will say to God that we have done our best. And then a great wave of mercy and compassion will sweep over us; and the stars in the sky will shine like diamonds for us. And we will be at peace. We will look back on this life, with all its suffering and hardship, and we will smile.

In discussing the concepts that creation is an ongoing and always evolving occurrence and that Jesus' historical mission on this earth was to teach us how to live, we also need to revisit our traditional view of the sacrament of baptism. We were taught that everyone is born with original sin on their soul, the mark of the sin of our first parents coming down to everyone through the act of procreation. The only way that this stain, this sin, could be wiped out was through baptism. Because of this belief we grew up with a sense of urgency in relation to infant baptism because we believed that a child who died without the sacrament could not enter heaven. This led to an even more damaging belief, happily never declared a doctrine of our faith, even if widely believed, that a child who died without baptism would go to a place called limbo, which was neither heaven nor hell, but some type of vague semi-existence. Here in Ireland, this spiritual no man's land was mirrored in the practice of excluding unbaptised infants from Christian burial grounds. The number of *cillíní* around the country are testament to our belief that these children were tarnished with sin and that we were all born into sin. I don't know if many believe much of that any more. Certainly the rush to have a child baptised is no longer happening, and parents often wait a few months, or even years, before having the ceremony. If we are to accept the idea of the divine presence in the work of continuing creation that I am outlining here, we believe that we are not born into sin, but into the love of the creator. We are born into life, not death, into love, not separation, and the purpose of the sacrament of baptism changes. It now becomes an outward sign of welcoming the child into the believing community, the followers of Jesus, no more or less than that. This, of course, assumes that the community is a real live believing entity. It is a good many years now since Matthew Fox wrote in *Original Blessing* that, rather than being born in a state of sin, we are each of us brought into being by the Divine Creator in an act of love, so that our existence is blessed from the very first moment. He posits the idea of original blessing rather than original sin. As is often the case, poets can convey these thoughts with more imagination than the rest of us. In 'Intimations of Immortality' Wordsworth says that we come into this world 'trailing clouds of glory', and that 'heaven lies about us in our infancy'. In other words, we come into this world in a state of purest innocence and it is hard to look upon a newborn child and not believe this.

I know that what I am writing here might pose problems for people who are content and happy in the faith in which they were brought up, and who have developed a relationship with God the Father in the traditional understanding of him sitting on his throne in heaven. Maybe people like that will have given up on this book at this stage. I believe that our generation has lived through an extremely traumatic time in the history of our Church. By and large most of us also had the opportunity of education – we have read widely throughout our lives and have been exposed to a great variety of ideas. This in itself is good, and it helps to broaden our minds, but it also challenges many of the assumptions we previously took for granted. I find that many of my generation of Catholics are full of questions and uncertainties. I think that, apart from clarifying my own views, which is always one of the benefits of writing, I am writing for these other people, people for whom the old answers are no longer adequate, people whose adult children can no longer accept the neat dogmas that we were taught. There are many who have studied widely in other fields but whose theological development has not progressed in our Church. They know that the literal interpretation of the Bible can no longer hold. In all of this, it is important to recognise that while the Word of God cannot always be taken as historical fact, it contains truth – the deeper meaning that is to be found in the figurative, imaginative language. In so far as I have come to new understandings, I know that I am groping on the other side of the veil; I am not so much rejecting the past, but standing back from it and beginning to grasp it in new and more meaningful ways. I want to share this with anyone who may find it helpful. I do believe that we are living through what some have called a tectonic shift, and what Hans Küng calls a paradigm shift, which he says happened historically about every 500 years, or what Australian writer Michael Morwood calls the time of the greatest theological shifts ever. The essence of this type of dramatic change or shift is that it demands new ways of thinking, new ways of looking at old truths in order to breathe new life into them that will make them credible for a new age. Our Christian tradition is a rich one and we have an obligation to communicate it to the generations who are coming after us.

Karl Rahner, one of the great theologians of the last century, says, 'Our present situation is one of transition ... to a Church made up of those who have struggled against their environment in order to reach a personally clear and explicitly responsible decision of faith. This will be the Church of the future or there will be no Church at all.'

In *Blue Sky God* D. McGregor puts it another way: 'In the Western world, huge numbers of people have walked away from the traditional, doctrinal, overarching story offered by the institutional Christian Church – and that is very sad as it actually has so much to offer if only it could escape from its straightjacket of doctrine and liturgy.'

That, as I see it, is the challenge, to escape from the straightjacket of doctrine and liturgy.

To sum up, I am not suggesting that Jesus of Nazareth was not the Son of God. He undoubtedly had a very special relationship with the being he called Father. But I am suggesting that maybe by calling Jesus the only Son of God we might be putting him into a different and separate category from the rest of humanity. I am proposing that we look on the divine presence in creation in a new way, in a way that allows us to see ourselves, also, as sons and daughters of God. So maybe Jesus is more like us, and we like him, than we traditionally believed. Is it possible that all of us, in some profound and mysterious way, are both human and divine?

4

Mary's Place in the Church

When discussing aspects of Church doctrine to which many people of this age are not able to give full assent, consideration must be given to the Church's teaching on Mary, the mother of Jesus. We are asked to believe that she was born without stain of original sin, as a result of what is called the immaculate conception, that she was and remained a virgin all her life, that she conceived her son Jesus not by human means but through the direct intervention of the Holy Spirit, and that she had no further children; also that on her death she was taken up – assumed – body and soul into heaven. Added to these are the proclamations of Mary as Mother of God and Mother of the Church. What is most striking about all of this is that if you omit the nativity narratives, which most scholars of the Bible now accept are not historical, there are only a few very brief mentions of Mary in the gospels. We meet Mary, the mother of Jesus, in just a couple of stories and the content of these stories does not add credence to most of the doctrines that the Church teaches.

When Jesus was twelve years old he went up to the Temple in Jerusalem with 'his parents' to celebrate the Passover. Luke's Gospel tells us that Mary and Joseph realised that he was not with the family as they returned home. They went back to Jerusalem and searched for him for three days, until they eventually found him in the Temple. It is Mary who rebukes Jesus, asking how he could have done this to them – how he could have been so thoughtless, and did he not realise how worried his father and herself had been about him. When Jesus said that he must be about his father's business, we are simply told they did not understand. It is significant that in this gospel passage we are told that Joseph and Mary are parents of Jesus, and Mary refers to Joseph as the father of Jesus.

In the account of the marriage feast of Cana we are told that Jesus and his mother were present, that the wine ran short and that Mary brought this to the attention of her son. His response to her can be paraphrased as 'that has nothing to do with me, and anyway the timing is not right'. This account of the marriage feast would have been handed down through the oral tradition and the account of the incident is found only in John's Gospel, which was finally written down about AD 100 or so. The community that had gathered around John was developing a theology of the Eucharist, so it is possible that the focus of the author of this story was on the wine as a Eucharistic symbol and may not have been overly concerned with the mother–son interaction. Either way, Mary is reported as telling the stewards to do whatever Jesus told them to do, and following the event he went 'down to Capernaum with his mother and the brothers'. The Church has not inferred any doctrinal teaching from this episode, but it has been widely and freely used in pastoral settings, spiritual writing and preaching to paint a picture of Mary as the one who is most successful in interceding with Jesus when we are praying for some favour. There could almost be a misrepresentation of Mary going back and forth with our petitions, as if with her help we could change the mind and will of God. I don't intend here to dismiss the practice of praying for our needs or for the needs of others, though in another place in the gospels Jesus is quoted as saying that God the Father knows our needs before we ask, which would seem to indicate that there is no necessity to list them. I believe that when we pray for people we are wishing them well, we are entering into and expanding the creative love of the Divine, who is present in all of creation and is pouring his loving care on all. So my prayer becomes part of the all-encompassing care of God. The other thing to be said about the Cana episode is that it portrays Mary as someone who was empathetic to the human, ordinary needs of people and was prepared to search for a solution, and in this way she can be seen as a model of caring and kindness. The episode also depicts Jesus as engaging in very ordinary human behaviour – attending a wedding in the company of his mother and his kin – and points to Mary as a fairly typical woman of her time.

Possibly the most telling incident concerning Mary is Matthew's account of Jesus coming back to preach in the synagogue of his home town of Nazareth. The people listening to him want to know the source of his wisdom. They know his seed and breed. For them he is the carpenter's son, his mother is a woman called Mary and the author names his four brothers, James, Joseph, Simon and Judas, and says that he has sisters, though they are not named. This raises questions about the perpetual virginity of Mary and it is clear this constituted a problem for the theologians and teachers who were defining doctrines during the first few centuries of the Church. They taught, for reasons that had to do with prevailing attitudes towards women and sexual relationships in that era, that it would make the whole notion of Jesus being the exclusive Son of God more credible if it was maintained that Mary had remained a virgin all her life. As a consequence the standard explanation offered in Church circles for this passage was that the words for brother, sister and cousin were interchangeable in a society where extended families were the norm, so we could take it that these people mentioned as Jesus' brothers and sisters were in fact cousins, Jesus was an only son and Mary a perpetual virgin. Even in my young days, before I ever studied theology, I considered that to be a fairly obvious ploy to try to make sense of a doctrine whose foundations were shaky, to say the least. At this stage of my life, what is important for me is the realisation that Mary was a very significant person in Jesus' life, and her holiness does not depend on whether or not she was a virgin.

Mark's Gospel was the first of the four gospels to be written and, as such, is considered to be the closest to an eye-witness account of the life of Jesus. In this gospel we are told of an occasion where Jesus' relatives set out 'to take charge' of him, convinced that he was out of his mind. Mary is not specifically mentioned here, but it is a reasonable assumption that she shared this concern. Was she anxious about the behaviour of her son, and did she want to bring him back under the control of the family? If so, it would be a very human reaction. Three of the gospels tell us of a time when Jesus is informed that his mother and his family are looking for him. The story doesn't say that Jesus agreed to see them. Instead, we are told that he responds by saying that his kin, his family, are those who live by the word of God, who do the will of the

Father. There is a suggestion of an estrangement between mother and son, between Jesus and his siblings. This suggestion is further amplified in Mark's account of his return to Nazareth, mentioned above. We are told that the people did not accept Jesus and he sounds weary as he declares that a prophet is only despised in his own country, among his own relations and in his own house. In these passages there is an implication of a tension in the mother–son relationship, again, not an unusual phenomenon in many of our own families.

I find it difficult to write about the place of Mary in our faith. I spent a great part of my priestly life conducting popular devotions to Our Lady, under the title of Our Mother of Perpetual Help. Thus I have had ample evidence of how much she means for many Catholic believers. I think it is true to say that a large part of popular devotions are directed more to Our Lady than to God. Among traditional Irish Catholics there is a warmth and ease of relationship with Mary that is stronger than their feelings about God or even Jesus. As a Redemptorist I have been up and down the country conducting novenas to Our Lady, and for many years the word 'novena' attached to an event was enough to ensure large and enthusiastic crowds. There are also many places around the world where Mary is believed to have appeared to people, and in some of them delivered messages for the world. Irish people have flocked to places like Lourdes, Fatima and Medjugorje, along with our own pilgrimage place at Knock, County Mayo.

So what do I now believe about Mary, the mother of Jesus? I accept the general understanding of scholars that the stories of the conception and birth of Jesus are mythological rather than historical. They feature in the gospel accounts of Matthew and Luke, but not in Mark or John, or in the writings of St Paul, and Paul's writings are considered earlier than any of the gospel accounts. These myths are not unique to the Christian story, but bear a striking resemblance to many ancient myths about gods and the children of gods, and about gods coming down and having sexual relationships with women on earth. The aim of the nativity story was to reinforce the belief that Jesus was the long-promised Messiah, and this belief had to be spread among Jews and non-Jews or Gentiles alike. Paul, in the letters he wrote to the various communities to whom he had preached and which have come down to us in the Bible, emphasised and promoted the idea of Jesus of Nazareth as the Christ, the expected and long-awaited saviour of the Jews. The problem that the early preachers of the message of Jesus faced, when they presented Jesus as the fulfilment of the promise of the Old Testament – in other words as the Messiah, the Chosen One, the one sent by God – was the nature of his death. He died as a criminal, and this presented a quandary to anyone attempting to convince people that he was the Messiah. Furthermore, as the preaching about Jesus and his message began to spread into the Greek and Roman worlds, something more miraculous was needed in the origin of Jesus to make him more believable for the Greeks. Matthew, on the other hand, was writing for the Jews, so his concern was to make the story of Jesus' birth match the prophecies of the Jewish Bible. It is probable that for reasons like these a myth developed around the origin of Jesus of Nazareth, which we now know as the nativity narratives.

Does that mean that these stories are false, and the writers were telling lies? No, it is rather a matter of understanding different times, and different ways of communication. We live in a time when we tend to take things literally; what is written down is to be understood as historical fact, as an actual description of what happened. The people who lived around the time of Jesus, and the early chroniclers of his life, had a different understanding. They were more in tune with the world of mystery than we are; they understood that there is another reality beyond what we can see, hear, feel and know through our senses. That world of mystery is beyond the grasp of our understanding, of our explaining. The only way we can begin to reach into it is through story, through metaphor and myth. I expect the early believers, the readers of the first drafts of what we now know as the New Testament, knew how to interpret these stories of the coming of Jesus on earth. They knew not to take them as literal descriptions of historical events, but rather to look behind the story to the message it contained. And the message they would have taken from these stories was about who Jesus was, not about how exactly he was born. They would have understood that Jesus of Nazareth was, according to the writer, a messenger from God, from the Divine, sent to bring them a new understanding of life, a new way of living, which he referred to as the kingdom of God. It was his life and his message that were important, not the details of his conception and birth.

This in no way means that we should not celebrate Christmas. The wonder of Christmas is one of the positive features of our faith. All of us who believe in Jesus of Nazareth can happily celebrate his coming into the world and listen to the Scripture readings, even if we have different interpretations of the stories around his birth. Let those who believe that what we read in the gospels is exactly how it happened continue to do so. But for Ó Murchú's wise elders, I think we need something more credible, something that opens us up more to the presence and wonder of the workings of the Divine now in our own lives and in creation. And that is where stories as metaphor speak more profoundly to us – the possibility that the Divine can intervene in the ordinary circumstances of our lives. After all, Joseph and Mary were said to be going to Bethlehem on very run-of-the-mill business – registering for the census. In the mundane events of our lives, God's plan for us, for the world around us, can come to fruition.

In an earlier chapter, I raised questions concerning our traditional understanding of original sin – and proposed that we do not come into this world with the stain of sin but, rather, we come full of God's love. If we take this perspective on original sin, the dogma of the immaculate conception of Mary contains difficulty for us. If we reject the notion that God punished all of humanity because of the sin of our first parents and the further corollary that this sin was inherited by everyone, then the idea that any of us were born with original sin no longer makes sense. At the risk of repeating myself, I now believe that creation is a present and ongoing reality rather than a single historical event, a reality eternally underpinned, guided and sustained by the divine presence, and I cannot believe that God was absent from the lives of humanity and all creation from the beginning until the saving death of Jesus. I now believe that all of creation, including myself, you the reader, Mary the mother of Jesus, and all humankind, is born into love, created and upheld by the love of the Divine Spirit, and in no way cut off from God's love by sin, either our own or that of our first parents. St Paul, writing to Timothy, says, 'we may be unfaithful, but he is always faithful, for he cannot deny his own self'. I believe that if we apply this understanding to Mary's immaculate conception we can conclude that all of us are equally immaculately conceived by love, imbued with the life of God which is manifested in every newborn baby from the moment of birth. This is not to say that our world is free from sin – it would be a very foolish person who would posit such a theory – but we are not born with sin, rather we choose actions that are contrary to the love into which we are born. I believe that human nature is flawed and that, as we go through life, there is always a struggle going on within each one of us – the struggle between virtue and vice, between decency and decadence, between unselfishness and selfishness. We don't always act as agents of love for ourselves, our fellow humans or the planet. I believe that Mary's birth was no different from that of the rest of us, but I want to believe that she acted more as an agent of love than we do. That is enough for me.

Was Mary assumed body and soul into heaven? I don't know if she was but at a time when it was believed that she was taken up to heaven, the earth was considered to be flat and to be the centre of the universe and bounded by the sky. In an effort to make meaning of life after death, it was plausible to accept the notion of a heavenly dwelling somewhere above, beyond the moon and the stars. That type of idea doesn't fit as easily with us now, nor does the idea of our bodily presence being replicated in whatever our eternity turns out to be. It is good to remember that the dogma of the Assumption was not proclaimed by the Church until the 1950s, and it has no foundation in Scripture. It is based on a tradition that dates back to the seventh century. The feast is celebrated on 15 August, and for many Catholics it has become a significant date in the summer calendar. It can bring a spiritual dimension into people's lives as we move towards the end of summer. In Ireland we have the tradition of visiting blessed wells dedicated to Mary on that day, and I believe that these wells are holy places. They are holy because of the tradition of prayer and dependence on the Divine associated with their locations. When we spend time at such places, we are following an ancient tradition and often experience a sense of oneness within ourselves, with others and with God. In my local town it is the day that people gather at the well, Mass is celebrated, people walk in circles around the well and recite prayers, and there is a weekend of festivities. It marks the shortening of the days as the summer nears its end and the harvest is at hand. We can honour Mary on this date without necessarily believing she was assumed, body and soul, into heaven. We can treat this doctrine as a myth or metaphor that points to a belief that there is a life beyond this present existence.

So where does that leave the modern believer as regards devotion to Our Lady? I tend to assume that a major reason for the popularity of devotion to Mary in Catholic spirituality had to do with the distant, remote and often angry and forbidding image we had of God. That image of God has its origins in a church that was modelled on the structure of the Roman Empire, and later on the pattern of medieval princes and kings. What these had in common was that the emperor or king was a remote and powerful figure, and there was no way that the ordinary subject could approach the throne directly. God was pictured as someone who was equally powerful and remote, and could not be approached, a remote figure on a throne in some distant dwelling in the sky, so an intermediary was essential. Mary, as the mother of Jesus, fitted perfectly into this category. Since God was far too magisterial for us lowly beings to approach, we turned to Mary to intercede for us. The titles 'Mary, the Mother of God' and 'Mary, the Mother of Jesus' became interchangeable, and it is fair to say that our notions of Mary's roles as intercessor were jumbled in our psyche. One time we were harking back to Cana where she is pleading for us with her son, and another time we were asking her to approach God on our behalf. This God on the throne was seen as someone who was monitoring our every action. Unfortunately, as Catholics, we did not take account of the psalmist's image of God, someone who is 'slow to anger and rich in mercy'. Many of us saw God as stingy with mercy and forgiveness, granting it only on condition that we made a 'good' confession that entailed a 'firm purpose of amendment'. Our God was someone to be feared and the divine presence was not experienced as something that was sustaining and loving. It was much easier to trust in the kindness of a mother to help us out and, in the process, we formed a distorted image of Mary, an image that was not based on Scripture and one to which many women could not relate. If we base our image of Mary on the episodes in the gospels we find an ordinary woman. She was a worried mother when she was separated from her son, and she reprimanded him, though not harshly, not in a manner that would damage his self-esteem. There is a strong suggestion that she was still a worried mother when she came looking to have a word with him during his public ministry. We get the impression that, at least to some extent, she did not understand him and his mission.

Down through the years, when other colleagues and I conducted very popular novenas to Our Lady, one of the big features was the writing of petitions. We encouraged people to write out their petitions and thanksgivings to Mary, and at each session a number of these would be read out. Looking back from my current perspective I can see that the whole notion of encouraging people to write prayers of petition to Mary was a very doubtful practice and promoted a false sense of the Divine and a mistaken understanding of prayer. Certainly, during the 1970s and 80s, when the novena movement was at its height, the focus on written petitions was, I believe, seriously flawed. Petitions were read out asking Mary to cure diseases, help people to pass exams, ensure a happy death and intervene in all the various vicissitudes of life. Neither life, nor prayer, work that way. As time went on an effort was made to present Mary as the mediator by encouraging people to begin their petitions with the phrase, 'Dear Mary, please ask your Son to … ', but I don't know how effective that was. In the context of the whole event it was a small gesture towards a better theology, though it must be said that the homily more often than not attempted to counteract the tendency to over-exaggerate the role of Mary. I write this to acknowledge my own role in promoting an unreal notion of Mary and to recognise that such promotion may have actually brought prayer and religious practice into some disrepute. I fully accept that devotion to Mary has its place within Catholic spirituality. The Marian shrine pilgrimages and the various novenas and other devotions have sustained many people in their faith and have been occasions of communal prayer. The recitation of the Rosary, especially at times of illness and death, expresses our dependence on God, our awareness that we are not entirely the authors of our own individual destiny. That is the key concept in all forms of prayer, including Marian devotion – our reliance on God who knows our needs even before we express them. What is really important is that we do not claim that these devotions are the only way of praying and that people who do not practise them are less Catholic or, indeed, less worthy.

It is possible that, in some people's understanding, what I am saying may be seen as unorthodox and might be disturbing. I have no wish to rob anyone of their beliefs, but we are now living in a new reality. Our present age is an extraordinary time of change. We are part of what Hans Küng described as a paradigm shift, a radical change that has occurred historically only every 500 years or so, a time when we see things in a totally new way. For so many people today religious belief has lost all meaning. We desperately need to find new concepts and new language to present the message of Jesus of Nazareth in a way that communicates to the modern mind and heart. One of the themes of this book is that I believe the Church has made a big mistake down through the ages, and maybe most especially in the earlier centuries. The mistake was to encase its particular understanding of the life and message of Jesus into rigid defined doctrines that were to be held by all believers for all time. This did not allow for the development of thought and doctrine. We are now faced with a dilemma. How can we break out of the straightjacket of rigid doctrine, which we clearly see does not communicate effectively any more, and set the Christian message free for a new time? In this chapter I have been attempting to open up some new ways of looking at Mary, the mother of Jesus, ways that might mean more to the people of our time who are struggling with their beliefs. If we can begin to recognise the presence of the Divine sustaining our existence in love, perhaps we won't feel the same need for a mediator, and we can begin to look at Mary, the mother of Jesus, in a different way. We can see her as a human being, a mother and a wife, who struggled with all the same problems as any woman in a relationship and rearing a family. In this way she can become for us less of a remote, heavenly figure and more of a real flesh-and-blood human person who lived life much as we ourselves have to live it.

5

The Church's Fatal Flaw: Exclusion of Women

*A*mong the many problems facing the Catholic Church, granting full equality to women in both leadership and ministry will be one of the most difficult to resolve, and at the same time it is, I believe, the most essential issue that has to be tackled. I think it is probably true that the future credibility of the Catholic Church will depend to a great degree on its willingness to accord women full parity with men. Facing up to its treatment of women is as important as acknowledging its failures regarding clerical sex abuse, and I believe that both subjects are interrelated.

In today's milieu, particularly in the developed world, equality for women is more and more accepted as the norm in government, in business and in society generally, though sometimes it is honoured more in theory than in practice. I have no doubt some women would tell me that there still is a fair way to go before full equality is achieved, but things have improved to a point where few people would argue against the principle of equality at least. People disagree about whether the quota system is a good way to achieve equality, for instance in political representation, while others argue that women's sport doesn't get its fair share of media coverage, but it would be rare enough now to meet someone in the developed world who would argue against the idea of gender equality in principle. The exception is the Catholic Church, where women are still excluded from ordination and from any significant involvement in decision-making, because all authority in the Church is securely hitched to ordination to the priesthood, and only males are eligible for that. Within the membership of the Church there is no shortage of people who will take a vehement stand against gender equality, and do so without any sense of doubt or shame, in fact with total conviction. The amazing thing is that it is not only men who take this stand – some women do also.

The Church has a long history of marginalising women, which many people have written about, including myself in a previous book. I think it is no exaggeration to say that misogyny has been prevalent in the Church at least from the third century down to our own time. Catholic theology and spirituality have been shaped through the centuries almost exclusively by men. A few women, like Teresa of Avila and Catherine of Siena, have been recognised as Doctors of the Church, but they were the exceptions. Other brilliant and deeply spiritual women, like Hildegard of Bingen, Mechthild of Magdeburg and Marguerite Porete, were persecuted and their writings suppressed, though Hildegard has been given full recognition in recent years. Poor Marguerite suffered the ultimate fate, having been condemned and burned at the stake by the notorious Inquisition. A fuller account of the writings of this woman can be found in Mary T. Malone's excellent book *The Elephant in the Room: A Woman's Tract for Our Times*.

Both theology and spirituality have been much the poorer for the lack of feminine insight, and this lack has given rise to a Church where patriarchy is rife. For at least the whole of the past millennium, authority systems and structures in the Church had achieved almost supernatural status, being viewed with reverence as drawing their authority directly from God, and, as a result, people in the Church were generally very docile and obedient. 'Father knows best; His Lordship knows even better; His Holiness is infallible.' But that has all changed in our lifetime. We are now living in a much more questioning time, with a more sceptical view of authorities generally, and particularly in the Catholic Church. I think it is fair to say that the Church has to a large extent brought this decline in respect for its authority on itself. It began at the Second Vatican Council in the middle of the last century, when the council re-established the primacy of the individual conscience, which led people to at least begin to have some trust in their personal judgement about matters to do with their own lives. This was, in itself, a very good development, but considering that most people had little or no experience of exercising their conscience, it needed follow-up education and support to give people confidence in this new way of looking at things. Then along came *Humanae Vitae* in 1968, an encyclical that reinforced the ban on the use of artificial contraception. The large majority of Catholics rejected the teaching contained in that encyclical, and still do to this day. The message of *Humanae Vitae* really affected women and the vast majority decided to follow their conscience.

However, Church leadership retaliated with a new line, namely that people could only follow their conscience if they had gone to the trouble of informing this conscience, and the guide on this road to an 'informed conscience' was Church teaching. People saw through this catch-22 and made their own decision on a deeply intimate aspect of their lives. Having rejected one facet of Catholic moral teaching, people began to question more teachings. Then the clerical sex abuse issue became public, particularly the efforts by authorities to cover it up. The result of all this is a great lessening of respect and credibility for what popes, bishops and priests have to say. So when a pope or a bishop declares nowadays that women can never be ordained to the priesthood in the Catholic Church, people are quick to challenge and contradict him. Pope John Paul II tried to silence opinions and discussion on this topic by declaring, in the 1994 document *Ordinatio Sacerdotalis*, that women could never be ordained, and that this teaching was definitive and for all time.

The regime of Pope John Paul II was fairly intolerant of difference; many of us still remember his finger wagging at Ernesto Cardenal. Clergy and people in theological positions in seminaries and universities were slow to challenge his edicts and, consequently, his declaration that the matter of women's ordination to the priesthood could not even be discussed initially had a considerable impact. Many people became very cautious about even mentioning the topic, because the penalties at the time were very severe. Pope Benedict followed up by emphasising what he termed 'the definitive' nature of John Paul's teaching, so that, while not exactly going as far as to declare it infallible, he went as close as he conceivably could. In the process he created a certain confusion between what he called definitive teaching and the more traditional notion of infallible teaching. Calling something a 'definitive teaching' was a new concept in the Church, and I suspect the Vatican were slow to explain clearly what it meant, hoping that they could tough it out by leaving it slightly vague. But one thing was certain, we were left in no doubt that the sanctions for disobeying this 'definitive teaching' would be severe, a fact to which I can personally testify. Proclaiming that John Paul's teaching was 'definitive' had the effect of stopping the debate in official Church circles for a number of years, with theologians, bishops and priests largely avoiding the topic. It wasn't that the more liberal ones kept away from the subject entirely. They were careful in the way they kept circling around it, writing and speaking about the crisis in priesthood due to the shortage of priests, suggesting that priests who left to get married could be invited back into ministry, even calling for the ordination of married men, as had happened in the early Church. Some still ventured into the dangerous territory of women's place in the Church, suggesting that there should be more women in positions of decision-making, even hinting at women as deacons. But the words 'women' and 'ordination' were rarely joined together in any of the theological books or magazines of that time. A couple of theologians, like Jacques Dupuis and Tissa Balasuriya, or priests like Roy Bourgeois, did venture into this territory, and lost their jobs or were suspended. In Australia Bishop Bill Morris said that if the Church approved of the ordination of women, he would be willing to perform such a ceremony. On the face of it, what he said was unobjectionable, but the paranoia about the matter was such that he was sacked. Some other bishops spoke up, but only after they had retired, which I always thought was a little bit unconvincing; it is regrettable that these men did not speak out while still in office. One thing is sure; it was a clear indication of the lack of freedom of expression within the system.

Church reform groups, and in particular women's groups, who had some theological or scriptural knowledge, were not silent and, unlike clerics and teaching theologians, they had no need to fear sanctions. They continued speaking out strongly, calling for ordination to be open to all, often using the phrase 'the equality of all the baptised'. The Vatican could deal with theologians and priests by imposing penalties on them, but to have widespread opposition to their teaching from increasingly vocal lay people with knowledgeable arguments was something new, and they did not know how to handle it. Official arguments against women's ordination were being shown up as weak, often without any real foundation. It was being suggested that a deep-seated misogyny was at the core of Church objections both historically and in the present time, and it was hard to counter that argument. The evidence suggesting the presence of misogyny was strong. Gradually fear of bringing up the subject was dissipating, and even Church people were getting more outspoken. I witnessed it myself in the Association of Catholic Priests. Initially we kept well away from the topic, despite the fact that the aggressively conservative 'Catholic' papers kept trying to corner us on the question, hoping to be able to use it against us by branding us as heretics. As time went on we too got more courage, and now it is part and parcel of what we mention when we speak about Church reform, maybe nuanced at times by putting the emphasis more on the equality of women in the Church, rather than specifically on their ordination to the priesthood. Perhaps a more important reason for the nuance is that an increasing number of us believe that the institution of priesthood itself needs to be substantially reformed before other changes are made. More people are expressing the reality that Jesus did not ordain anyone and are wondering what our Church would look like if we did not have 'priests'.

The election of Pope Francis brought about a new sense of openness in the Church. At an early stage he made it clear that he wished everyone to speak freely and without fear, and that he wanted to listen to people's opinions rather than silence them. Fear of sanctions because of views expressed decreased greatly, and though Francis himself is not in favour of the ordination of women to the priesthood (he asserts, with, I think, some degree of justification, that he does not wish to 'clericalise' women), the topic is now discussed more openly. One of the really bright lights in the Church at the moment, Vincent Long, Bishop of Parramatta in Australia, speaking on the topic of Church reform, said the following:

So long as we continue to exclude women from the Church's govern-ance structures, decision-making processes and institutional functions, we deprive ourselves of the richness of our full humanity. So long as we continue to make women invisible and inferior in our Church's language, liturgy, theology and law, we impoverish ourselves as if we heard with only one ear, we saw with only one eye and we thought with only one half of our brain – and often the lowest reptilian section thereof. Until we have

> *truly incorporated the gift of women and the feminine dimension of our*
> *Christian faith, we will not be able to fully energise the life of the Church.*

While this is a very strong statement, even Vincent is careful not to mention the word 'ordination' in relation to women, even though everything he says implies either opening ordination to women or changing canon law in order to allow non-ordained people to have positions of authority in the Church. I don't know which of those two options the Church would find more difficult to stomach. But Vincent, being a bishop, presumably decided it was wiser for him not to spell out the implications of what he was saying, and risk drawing down the wrath of the Vatican on himself. He had the example of Bill Morris, his colleague in the Australian Church, demoted under Pope Benedict. Just as an aside, it is an interesting little detail that the person Pope Benedict sent to investigate Bill Morris was the recently retired archbishop of Philadelphia, Charles Chaput, who is now one of the most trenchant critics of Pope Francis. Bishop Chaput was one of the first to come out in support of Archbishop Viganò's public call for Francis to resign.

Opinion polls in this country regularly tell us that a large majority of regular church-going Catholics are in full agreement with having women ordained as priests. A poll of farmers, often regarded (rightly or wrongly) as the most traditional sector of Irish society, was taken at the National Ploughing Championships and it showed that they too are strongly supportive of the priesthood being open to women.

It is worth looking at the arguments put forward to justify the ban on ordaining women as priests. The traditional line was always to quote the example of Jesus. He chose twelve apostles, who were the first priests, ordained at the Last Supper, and they were all men. The conclusion drawn from that was that Jesus had decided for all time that priesthood was to be confined to men. End of argument. Now that we are in a more questioning age, people see many holes in the argument. Jesus was a Jew. All his apostles were Jews and he preached his message to the Jews. If the logic applied to gender was applied to race, then only Jewish men could be priests. On a more serious note, the only priests in the Jewish religion in Jesus' time were the men who served in the Temple in Jerusalem and Jesus didn't have a good relationship with them. It was the chief priest who was mainly responsible for putting him to death. The main religious officials of his time were the Pharisees who served in the synagogues in the towns and villages of Judea. Jesus is on record as being very critical of them. He was in every sense a non-institutional person. Is it likely that Jesus, at the very time when he was in a deadly struggle with the priests of his day, would ordain his followers as priests? It is also worth noting that the gospel accounts of the Last Supper were written many years after the death of Jesus, and the decisions on what would be included in and excluded from the New Testament as we know it were not finalised for another few hundred years, usually considered to be during the reign of Constantine in the early fourth century. By that time a combination of Greek philosophy and Roman political structures meant that a 'men only' ethos had become established in the burgeoning Christian Church. We know that at the Last Supper they were celebrating the annual Jewish Passover meal. It is most unlikely that such a meal would have been celebrated without the presence of women and children. The question remains, Why does the account that we have inherited suggest that there were only men present? An early example of the exclusion of women?

The other traditional argument that is used against the ordination of women is that the priest, standing at the altar celebrating Mass, is taking the place of Jesus. And since Jesus was male, only males can properly fulfil this role. This is a quite extraordinary argument that I believe lacks any credibility. Jesus represented the Divine in his full humanity, not in his particular gender. Surely it is absurd in the extreme to suggest that males are created more fully in the image of the Divine than females, which is the clear implication of that argument.

Many scholars now dismiss these traditional arguments at a more fundamental level by stating that Jesus did not ordain anyone, either at the Last Supper or at any time in his life. (This is the opinion that I expressed in a magazine about ten years ago, which led to my removal from priestly ministry.) In fact, priesthood developed slowly in the early Church over the first couple of hundred years. Jesus did choose the twelve apostles, usually interpreted as representing the twelve tribes of Israel, but choosing men at the time was more a reflection of social reality than gender preference. A reading of the gospel accounts of the life of Jesus from a feminine perspective shows clearly that Jesus was close to many women, and that some of them were leading members among his group of followers. The part Mary Magdalene played in the life and ministry of Jesus is being re-examined; it suggests that she had a particularly close relationship to him, and was one of the leading apostles. It is worth asking why the part she played was largely airbrushed out of the official accounts that have come down to us. She has been greatly maligned in popular Catholic belief, being presented, without any clear evidence, as a prostitute.

Pope Paul VI set up a commission to consider if the matter of women's ordination was decided by Scripture. When this commission reported in 1976, it concluded that there was no definite scriptural prohibition of the ordination of women, and that the question remains open. It also stated that there is nothing in Scripture that allowed for the ordination of women. This is hardly surprising, given that there is nothing in Scripture that states that Jesus ordained anyone. The argument about the maleness of Jesus was never very convincing. The significant reality about Jesus is not his maleness, but his humanity. Females share the humanity of Jesus just as surely and completely as males do. Still, the Church authorities held on to these arguments right down through the centuries to our own time, and they are still being trotted out by various bishops and theologians. Very few people give any credence to this view anymore.

Maybe because of this scepticism among believers a new argument has recently been presented to back up the ban on ordaining women. The idea of complementarity was presented in John Paul II's *Ordinatio Sacerdotalis*, and has also been quoted on a number of occasions by Pope Francis. The concept of complementarity is a complicated one, which I will try to explain briefly and simply, in so far as I can grasp it myself. The best clarification of this concept that I have come across was by Jeanne M. Follman, an American theologian who wrote a three-part essay, 'The Catholic Hierarchy's Problem with Sex', in *La Croix* Catholic magazine. The idea behind this theory of complementarity, as she illustrates it, is that men and women are innately different, but in their difference they complement each other. I don't think anyone would argue with the fact that men and women are different, but John Paul II pushed this argument to a new level by stating that the difference between the sexes is God-given and universal. Both he and Francis referred to what they called 'feminine genius', meaning the particular qualities that women possess. They enumerate four such qualities: women are receptive by nature, both in their physical make-up and their emotional and intellectual life; they are sensitive, and that leads them to be compassionate towards others; they are generous, especially in giving of themselves and their time to others; and they are maternal.

These are the qualities that make them innately suited to building homes and rearing children. God has made them this way, so that they can be the home-makers, and ensure the upbringing of the next generation. The God-given qualities of men, according to this notion of complementarity, have more to do with physical and mental strength, leadership and government.

The theological explanation that is presented around the complementarity theory outlines two dimensions of the human person. One is the Petrine dimension, based on the figure of St Peter, and it sets the context for masculine roles – apostles, bishops, priests, etc. – and the governance of the Church. The other is the Marian dimension, based on the person of Mary, the mother of Jesus, and it justifies a framework for maternal work. It suggests that the bearing and rearing of children, service to others and the general humanising of society is more peculiar to women. The complementarity argument posits that since men make up the Petrine dimension of the Church and women the Marian dimension, ordination to the priesthood and, following on from that Church governance, is reserved only to men. This, they say, is established by God.

This latest justification for the marginalisation of women in the Church is, in my view, no more credible that the traditional arguments. It smacks of a situation where an institution had an established policy, the justification for which was leaking credibility, and they were desperately trying to think up some new way to bolster their position. It is, yet again, the type of situation that the Church finds itself in due to the rigidity of its teaching. To quote Jeanne Follman:

According to this men and women must be different, must all be different, and their immutable complementary differences must go on to define and constrain what each individual is obligated to do, as well as that from which each is excluded. This view holds that there are only two sexes; that there are clear ways to distinguish them; that there is a fixed sexual essence which each member of the sex possesses; and that sex predicts individual behaviour.

This way of thinking about human beings, that each person is born with rigid and clearly defined sex differences, which make man and woman complementary, is out of touch with the modern understanding of the human person, with the reality of life, and with the way in which people live. The reality is much more fluid, even messy, and cannot be boxed into an abstract, rigid ideal. The qualities that the complementarity theory ascribes to women – receptivity, compassion, sensitivity, motherliness – are also available to men in greater and lesser degrees; just as the qualities of leadership, strength and decisiveness are clearly present in women, and significantly present in some. It is the same rigidity that is behind the Church's teaching on homosexuality and same-sex relationships. It views sexual essence as rigid and clearly defined. We are realising more and more that sex falls on a spectrum, that sexual boundaries are much more fuzzy than previously thought, and that not every individual has a clearly delineated sexual essence. This is all part of the knowledge we are acquiring through advances in science and in our understanding of human nature, and such awareness is making the rigid Church doctrines inherited from the past no longer credible. The argument that God dictates what a given person is and is not capable of, purely because of their gender, makes no sense to the modern mind. It stands in contradiction to so much that we now take for granted about human nature, and as such it is being widely rejected even within the Church. Across the world of government, science, business and media, women have shown themselves to be proficient performers, capable of leadership. Women are competent for priesthood.

I believe that change is happening in the Church, and is happening quickly, as more and more people are accepting that things cannot remain as they have always been. This change has been greatly facilitated by the policy of 'synodality' that is being pursued courageously by Pope Francis. By synodality he means creating forums in which the voices of more and more people are being heard. This inevitably leads to an opening of minds and the expression of ideas, and we can see this happening in relation to the place of women in the Church. The final document from the Synod on Youth (October 2018) talks about how women have been excluded from decision-making processes even when they 'do not specifically require ministerial responsibility'. It goes on to say: 'The absence of women's voices and points of view impoverishes discussion and the path of the Church, subtracting a precious contribution from discernment. The synod recommends making everyone more aware of the urgency of an inescapable change.'

'An inescapable change'. This is excellent, and it is an indication that some real change of mind and heart is actually going on at the centre of the Church. It is important to recognise that all change begins at the level of ideas, when some people begin to say out loud what many people are thinking. As this happens we see a growth in the number of people who accept the new thinking. The problem with the Catholic Church and ordination of women is that while the idea has been expressed for at least half a century and while the majority of Catholics now accept its validity, the Church is no nearer to executing the change. Furthermore, when some dioceses in Ireland have convened synods, those attending have been told that there is no point in reaching a decision to ordain women as Rome will not allow it. While the Synod on Youth spoke of the 'urgency of this inescapable change', there is one major obstacle, which they fail to mention, a clause in the Church's Code of Canon Law, Canon No. 129: 'Those who have received sacred orders are qualified according to the norm of the prescripts of the law, for the power of governance, which exists in the Church by divine institution and is also called the power of jurisdiction. Lay members of the Christian faithful can cooperate in the exercise of this same power according to the norm of law.' Sifting through the complex language, what this is saying simply and starkly is that in order to participate in governance in the Church a person must be ordained a priest. Lay people can cooperate, but cannot make decisions.

Consequently the situation is such that if the wish of the synod document is to be progressed one of two things has to change. Either the Church will have to lift the ban on women's ordination, or it will have to change Canon 129 of the Code of Canon Law, so that the power of decision-making within the Church will no longer be inextricably linked to ordination. Neither change would be easy. We can see how a simple matter, like the suggestion from a previous synod that divorced and remarried people could, in certain circumstances, be admitted to communion, caused such an uproar, and threats of schism. The traditional group among the senior members of the Church, who are well organised, will fight tooth and nail against any change that would allow greater participation of women in either ministry or decision-making. It will take very strong and decisive leadership in the Church to bring this about – realistically Pope Francis, while he is in many ways laying the groundwork, will not, in my opinion, be the one to give women equality in the Catholic Church.

6

Discovering that Religious Men and Women Were Abusing Children

*A*s a priest and a religious, I have had a very personal interest in the various forms of sexual and physical abuse involving Church people that have come to light over the past 25 years. I have little doubt that my opinions and attitudes on this subject are influenced by the life I have lived, and the people with whom I have shared my life. I am aware that my main focus should be on those who suffered at the hands of the priests and religious, but this does not blind me to the fact that what has been revealed is a blight on the lives and ministry of priests, and has seriously damaged morale. It has caused great turmoil and upheaval in the Catholic Church. While institutional abuse by religious in places like mother and baby homes and laundries can at this stage be considered mostly a thing of the past in this country, since there are so few religious left, and they are mostly old, it is now clear that the revelations about clerical sexual abuse of minors will continue for a considerable time. When it first came to general notice in the 1990s, it was considered by some that this was a problem confined to countries in the western, developed world. But now stories are beginning to emerge out of South America, Africa and India, indicating that this is a worldwide problem in the Catholic Church, and that we are probably only at an early stage in learning the extent of it, and the level of damage that it has caused.

My involvement in two different elements of this story have influenced my thinking, and have even prodded me on occasions to tentatively challenge the prevailing consensus. When the *Ryan Report on Institutional Abuse* was published in 2009 I got a request from the then editor of Columba Press to know if I would be willing to edit a book of responses to it. I agreed to do so and quickly set about looking for contributors to the book. Since the institutions that were criticised in the report were run by religious – some brothers, but mostly sisters – I naturally went to speak to some of the religious sisters, to see what their reaction was, and if any of them would be willing to make a contribution to the book. A number were willing to speak to me, and tell me their side of the story, but none of them would venture to go public either in the forum I was providing, or in any other forum. By now we have become familiar with the hurt suffered by the inmates of these institutions, a great deal of which was completely inexcusable, but what I discovered was that a good number of sisters were also very hurt, even angry, at the way in which the investigation was conducted, and what they perceived to be the imbalance in media coverage. For instance, one sister told me of the allegation of abuse made against her by a person who had been a minor in an orphanage in which she had worked sporadically. When she was informed of the allegation – its nature, the time and place where it was reputed to have happened – she was horrified. She had good reason to be, since on that date she herself was a fifteen-year-old schoolgirl, living about 100 miles away from the place where she was reputed to have committed the offence. Despite years of effort, she never managed to get an acknowledgement that the allegation was false. Another sister told me about what was clearly an obviously false allegation against her (again, neither the date nor the location matched), so she went to the solicitor working for her religious community to explain the situation. The response she got from her solicitor, as she told it to me, was, 'Say nothing, and let him have his compensation.' These are just two examples of the type of stories I was hearing from religious sisters, many of whom were deeply angry and upset at what they perceived as a serious bias in the way the investigation was conducted. However, none of them would go public. Most of these sisters had lived quiet, unobtrusive lives working within their local community as teachers, nurses or social workers or in other community services. They didn't have, nor did they wish to have, any public profile. They were convinced that, if they went public, they would not be believed because of the prevailing atmosphere at that time, and that they would draw even more opprobrium on themselves. It is proper that the testimony of those who were resident in orphanages, laundries and reformatories are being heard and publicly acknowledged. It is also imperative to recognise that there is another dimension to this dismal chronicle that has not been told, and may never be recounted – the story of the religious sisters.

For the most part, religious congregations were founded to improve the lot of the poor and the deprived and their big mistake was to take on the task of dealing with problems that were rightfully the domain of society and of government. By doing so they became the controlling agents of society. It must be acknowledged that both state and society were by and large very happy to hand over these problems to them, and had a marked lack of interest in how they were being handled. It suited them to have what was then regarded as the unacceptable face of society locked away.

My second involvement in the world of clerical child abuse arose from my activity with the Association of Catholic Priests, of which I was a founding member in 2010. In retrospect, I think that founding this association was a somewhat more radical and controversial move than I or my co-founders realised at the time. I hadn't anticipated the reaction from authorities, or some of the Catholic media, to our intention to be an independent voice rather than an organisation that was under the jurisdiction of the bishops, as previous priests' councils had been. Our plan was to become a voice for priests at a time when, as a group, there was nobody to speak for them and when their morale was on the floor. As the stories of priests abusing children began to emerge, and as Church authorities were trying frantically to deal with it, or mostly to contain it and cover it up, a deep suspicion and, in some cases, alienation developed between priests and bishops, and many priests felt exposed and vulnerable. Our aim in founding the association was to promote reform in the Church according to the teaching of the Second Vatican Council, and we had not anticipated being a support for priests who had allegations of sexual abuse and inappropriate behaviour with minors made against them. To some extent this work cut across what we regarded as our real objective, to bring forward very necessary reforms. It demanded a lot of time and energy to unravel the facts of each case and, gradually, being a voice for priests around allegations of abuse became what we were most associated with in the public mind – some people did not always like to hear the complex reality of clerical child abuse. The media often parrot the phrase 'when you are explaining, you are losing'. In our case it seemed to be that when we were explaining, we were seen as, at best, defending, at worst, excusing.

The Association of Catholic Priests quickly got off the ground, and attracted far more members than we had expected. I still remember the enthusiasm of that first gathering in Portlaoise, where we launched the association. The hall we had prepared for the meeting quickly filled up, so we had to move to a much bigger location down the road. There was a real sense of excitement about that event, and it gave a great boost to the group who had initiated it. However, before long, priests who had accusations of child sexual abuse made against them began to contact us looking to us for support and help. In hindsight, we should not have been surprised by this. At that time the bishops, at local level, were terrified of media exposure and frightened of being on the wrong side of public opinion. In this climate of fear, the natural rights of the accused priest became casualties, particularly the right to one's good name. It became common practice for the bishop of a diocese to visit the parish and, during the celebration of the Eucharist, make known to the parishioners that an allegation had been made against the local priest. Using words like 'allegation' and 'alleged' did little to instil the dictum 'innocent until proved guilty' in people's minds. Prior to the public visit to the parish, the accused priest was summoned to the bishop's residence, often without being informed of the purpose of the meeting. In fairness, this apparent lack of concern for the rights of the priest was not due to malice. In my opinion, it was more a measure of the bishop's own anxiety in handling a situation that few of us would want to have landed on our desks. The upshot of all this was that the Association of Catholic Priests began to meet with priests whose lives were falling apart and who felt that they had no one to whom they could turn. Many were totally freaked out by the prospect of telling their own families and beset by the problem of how to account for the fact that they were not active in priestly work. We could see straight away that this was going to be difficult and complicated, and that we were not qualified to handle these cases. We managed to put together a legal team, willing to work for us pro bono, and at least now we had professional legal people to whom we could refer the accused priest.

In the early years of the association, it fell to my lot to be the main conduit between the accused priests and the legal team working for us. As well as the horror and revulsion of abuse, in addition to the damage done to people's lives by priests, a number of other factors came strongly to my attention. I learned that there was such a thing as a false allegation. This was difficult to deal with, because initially very few people, if any, were willing to accept that any allegation was false. Anyone who questioned the veracity of what the person making the accusation was saying was usually considered to be in denial about the reality of clerical child abuse. This was understandable to some degree, due to the secrecy and cover-up that surrounded this whole issue for so long, and also to the fact that most victims had never spoken about the abuse to anybody. For the most part, victims had not revealed the sexual exploitation to which they had been subjected because they felt an erroneous sense of shame and mistakenly saw themselves as somehow complicit in the loathsome acts that had been visited on them. As an association of priests, we were fortunate in that our solicitor was a really down-to-earth, clear-headed person, who could quickly sum up a case and decide if there was substance to the allegation against the priest. I learned over the years to trust this man's judgement, and he was seldom wrong. I must have come to know of at least a dozen instances of priests who were falsely accused during those years. Sadly, I also learned that the majority of allegations were true. Victims of abuse suffered great long-term damage, but at least now their stories were coming out and being believed. But for a priest to be falsely accused was the ultimate nightmare, not only for him but for his family and community. I know that a great many priests have lived with that fear for the past twenty years, knowing that all that was needed was one allegation, even if there was no truth to it, and they were automatically suspended from ministry. Even when the bishops gave up the practice of addressing the parish community, if the accused priest worked in a parish, or other public ministry, it would be next to impossible that the fact of an allegation of sexual abuse would not go public, leaving him with a long, uphill battle to clear his name. Gradually, as time went on, it began to be accepted that some allegations were false and better procedures were put in place to deal with this reality.

During those years, I encountered enormous layers of hurt: the hurt of priests and religious who often believed that all were tarred with the same brush; the sense of betrayal felt by faithful believers at the awful crimes committed by people they had looked up to; the hurt of Church authorities who now had to face the fact that they and their predecessors had been more concerned with the institution than with the truth; and most of all the hurt suffered by the victims of abuse. Something of what I began to realise during those years was put into words for me recently when I read what Bishop Vincent Long of Parramatta, Australia, said to a conference of priests in New Zealand: 'The sexual abuse crisis is inundating the whole Church like a tsunami and it has the potential to cause long-term damage, chaos and even schism. It is the biggest crisis since the Reformation and it exposes the ideological conflicts that run deeply through the length and breadth of the universal Church.'

Why did all this happen in the Catholic Church? Why did people who were in positions of great spiritual responsibility fail so badly, and do so much damage? Pope Francis said, 'It would be irresponsible not to go deep in looking for the roots and structures that allowed these evil acts to happen and simply to go on.' I will attempt here and in the following chapter to look into these deep roots as I see them.

I entered religious life in the early 1960s, and was ordained ten years later, so I think it is true to say that for my generation of priests, especially considering the years of change that we have lived through, dealing with sexuality was bound to play a big part in our lives. That is not to say that it didn't also play a big part in the lives of priests in previous generations, since human nature tends to be the same from one generation to the next. We were born into a time when the attitude to sex was that it was barely tolerable within the sacrament of marriage and its sole purpose was procreation. Then the 1960s came along, and throughout the years in which I was going through the formation system the whole attitude to sex and relationships changed dramatically in the world around us. No matter how enclosed or narrow our life might have been, there was no way we could completely escape being influenced by what was happening outside the boundaries of the seminary. In relation to sex, it can be the case that the less a person engages in it, the more it occupies their attention. I believe that for many priests, at a personal level, in our ministry, our social life and our relationships, we could not avoid having to struggle with sexual desires and attractions, in a clerical environment that provided us with few resources or understanding to help us along the way.

If I can extrapolate a little from my own experience, my siblings and I grew up and struggled through our teenage years, while society and moral attitudes were still dominated by the Catholic Church. My upbringing was sheltered – boarding school and at home during the holidays living out in the country, working on the farm and in the local commercial bog, and playing sport in the evening and at weekends. I didn't go to dances, and of course pubs were completely beyond consideration for me at the time. I am not sure that I even noticed girls very much. I have one clear memory of a fine summer evening in my teenage years when I was painting the gate leading from the house to the road. A local girl, a neighbour, was passing by and she stopped to chat. That must have made an impression on me, because I still have a very clear picture in my mind of that event. I know that my contemporaries, even in that small rural village, had a somewhat more adventurous adolescence than myself; anything up to eight young people would pack into a Volkswagen car and travel fifteen or twenty miles to a dance. I was not part of any such outing, probably because, even at that young age, I was already fingered for priesthood.

Even though the world outside Ireland was going through a dramatic change of attitudes and behaviour, liberation of any sort was slower to reach this country. Being in a seminary shielded us to some extent from what was happening around the world; there was no way we were going to San Francisco with flowers in our hair. Anyway, if I was typical of the young men in seminaries around the country at the time, it would take a whole garden full of flowers in my hair to even begin to loosen me out. I had no experience of having any serious conversation with anyone about sex – definitely not with my parents – and I don't even think that sex occupied my thoughts very much until I reached my twenties. I played a whole range of different sports at the time, and I suppose that absorbed a lot of my energy. But there is no doubt that guilt and fear were big factors in suppressing whatever sexual energy was developing during those years.

During my early seminary years in Galway I attended the university, doing an arts degree. Looking back now, I recognise that those were significant years for me. It was after the Second Vatican Council and things had become more relaxed in the seminary. There was more freedom to come and go, the cinema was not out of bounds and, after the first year or so, we didn't have to wear clerical attire in college. We were able to absorb some of the new attitudes that were spreading among the student body. Attending debates in the Literary and Debating Society certainly helped to broaden the mind, as for example when we witnessed Bishop Michael Browne being challenged by students in a way that he clearly did not expect and was uncertain how to handle. I know that a good number of the student body drank a fair deal during those years, but if there was a lot of sexual liberation I was totally unaware of it. I suspect there wasn't. Contraception was not available in Ireland at the time, and, as Bishop Doran of Elphin recently reminded us, the fear of pregnancy was a great deterrent. If young people were tempted to transgress in these matters, there was the further deterrent of having to go to confession and admit to your dalliance. Mass attendance in Ireland was over 90 per cent, and Church teaching still held sway, even among young people to a fair extent. Now, 50 years later, it is difficult to envisage a society that spoke of such things as 'mortal sin' and 'the sixth commandment'.

I believe that my generation of priests in Ireland came of age in an era of sensual and sexual suppression, living in an all-male seminary and imbued with negative teaching about sex and our bodies, while at the same time observing, and maybe even occasionally dipping our toe into a new atmosphere of freedom and liberation. It could be said that we were sexually at odds within ourselves. I can now see that it was a fairly hopeless environment in which to prepare for a life of celibacy, and if it was such for our generation it must have been even more so for the generations who had gone before us. The teaching of the Catholic Church was not questioned; therefore, it is perhaps no surprise that I have lived to see the Church facing possibly the greatest crisis of its long history, a crisis brought about by deviant sexual activity by its clerical class.

In our training we were told that celibacy was a privileged, indeed superior, way of life and that while it would cause some suffering and privation in this world, it would be generously rewarded in the next. We were also told that a celibate priest would be able to commit himself to his ministry and to the people he was serving much more than someone who had a wife and children. The writing of St Paul, of course, was used to back this up, where he wrote that the unmarried man was free to serve the Lord, whereas the married man had to serve his wife, the implication being that he would have less time and energy to serve God – a further example of the negative attitude to women so prevalent in the Church. The wife would come between him and God. If ever there was reference in our training to the longing of the human heart for love, we were told that the celibate priest would be in love with Jesus, and that was a deeper and more satisfying love than any human person could provide. The quote from St Augustine was often used to bolster that argument: 'You have made us for yourself, O Lord, and our hearts are restless until they rest in you.'

I recently heard an Irish bishop using both those arguments to justify celibacy, and they sounded stale and outdated to me, and completely out of tune with current understanding of the human person, which fully accepts the importance of relationship and intimacy in the life of all humans and acknowledges the fundamental connection between human love and love of God.

From the late 1960s the writings of Freud were making their way into our seminary libraries, but no Church official was questioning the celibacy rule. However, from the mid-1960s celibacy was being challenged by the actions of the many priests who left the ministry because they wanted to get married and raise a family. There was also an exodus from the seminaries, but even when confronted by these realities, Church leaders continued to maintain that celibacy was a prerequisite to priesthood. Coinciding with this demand that the priest must eschew sexual relationships there was the dreadful negativity of Catholic sexual teaching as a whole. While I remember reading about the dangers of repressed sexuality in my later seminary days, it obviously didn't impinge on me sufficiently to make me change my life direction. Now, almost 50 years later, these words from Robert Tracinski in the online publication *The Federalist* carry a much deeper meaning for me. The lessons of life!

When you attempt to totally suppress a normal and natural part of human life—and nothing could be more normal and natural than a desire to ensure the existence of our species in the first place—you are fighting a battle that you can't win. More specifically, when you try to suppress sexuality, it tends to come out sideways. Those who have no concept of a healthy sexuality will tend to develop an unhealthy sexuality. Hence the concentration within the Church hierarchy of men with a sexual preference for children and teenage boys.

If I had read this as a younger man, it is likely that I would not have accepted it as true. However, the revelations of the past 25 years concerning the sexual abuse of minors by clergy have convinced me of Tracinski's point of view. I am writing this in the aftermath of the report of sexual abuse by 300 priests in Pennsylvania since 1950, which, combined with our own Irish reports on clerical child abuse, dominated the visit of Pope Francis to this country. I am now convinced that there is something inherently injurious about compulsory celibacy. With the combination of hothouse seminary training, a negative and life-denying sexual doctrine, and the imposition of a life of celibacy, is it any wonder that a percentage of priests developed an unhealthy sexuality?

During the papal visit, some Irish bishops expressed the belief that here in Ireland we have got to grips with the problem, and that the worst is over. Certainly the Church here has put together a great deal of structures and regulations, under the general heading of 'Safeguarding', and there are much stricter, 'zero tolerance' attitudes towards any priest against whom a 'credible' allegation has been made. One high-ranking bishop even suggested that if the whole Church followed the Irish example, the problem would be solved.

Maybe it is true that all the efforts of the Irish Church have paid off. I am not convinced that structures, on their own, will resolve a problem that has its roots in arrested sexual development. Most of the revelations about clerical sexual abuse up to this point have come from countries in the developed world. We still have to hear about what has been going on in the global south, which is the area where Catholicism is growing and prospering at present. The indications are that when the full story comes out from places like Latin America, Africa and India, it will be just as problematic, perhaps more so. For instance, in 2002 a group of superiors of women's religious congregations in Africa sent a report to the Vatican outlining the abuse of their sisters by priests. The hints of what it contained were very disturbing; there were suggestions of male domination and entitlement, but the report was quickly and effectively suppressed, and, despite an occasional mention in the media, very little has been heard about it. All of that, and I suspect a lot more, will surely come to the light of day, which makes me believe that this problem of clerical sexual abuse will dog the Church for many years to come. A further feature of the story is also coming to light now – the fact that this type of behaviour is not confined to the lower ranks of the clergy, but seems to go right to the top, and even to persons closely linked with the Vatican itself. The stories of Marcial Maciel, founder of the Legionaries of Christ, who had children with at least two women, and was a serial abuser, abusing seminarians and priests in his own institute, and also his own children, and of Cardinal McCarrick of Washington, who is alleged to have used his position to abuse seminarians, are difficult for all of us in the Church to comprehend. In some ways the most disturbing of all is the revelation that Jean Vanier, who was regarded by many as a living saint, and who undoubtedly did good work, had sexually abused women. How could somebody combine that sort of abusive behaviour with occupying a senior, honoured position in the Church, or being looked up to by so many as a person of deep spirituality, even of great holiness? It brings home to us again the deep complexity of human nature, and the utter futility of setting people up as heroes or heroines, as great saints or great sinners. We are all flawed human persons, some more so than others, but nobody is perfect. Putting people on pedestals, as we often tend to do, inevitably leads to disillusionment. Only time will tell if we in the Church will be able to recognise and value the good that Jean Vanier did, while at the same time acknowledging that he did great damage to some women.

The main message I take from the recent revelations is that we must not ascribe to others great sanctity, any more than great sinfulness. I have seen the same reality over and over in my dealings with priests. I encountered men who did a lot of good, showed great dedication and commitment, and at the same time sexually abused minors. Is it at all possible for us to balance the fullness of a person's life, rather than dismissing them on the basis of one aspect of that life? I don't know. It is particularly hard when that one aspect involves the abuse of minors. Yet which of us would be able to hold our heads high if every detail of our lives was exposed to public view? No one is one-dimensional and the love of God embraces each one of us.

Putting all that aside, it is clear that the awful failure of the Church to deal with the widespread abuse of minors by clergy at all levels is a crisis of major proportions for the Catholic Church. Since we first began to get a hint of the enormity of this problem I have been frustrated by the response of Church authorities. I am not just referring here to the cover-up – that was probably the biggest failure of all and the one that was most alienating for the ordinary Catholic in the pew. Rather, I am considering the manner in which the Church authorities began to face up to the issue. In my view, they did not ask the right question: 'Why have priests, who profess to live by the gospel, sexually abused others?' Instead they put enormous effort into producing guidelines and setting up structures. All of these had their place, particularly the absolute directive that all crimes had to be reported to the civil authorities. There is also the law of unintended consequences, and we now have a situation where clerical child abuse has become quite a lucrative industry. Most dioceses and religious congregations employ professional staff, many of whom are retirees from the state sector, while at the same time little or nothing is expended on adult religious education or liturgy. My frustration has to do with the fact that there was little or no effort to look deeper, to try to recognise why these things happened, why people who had done long years of training and dedicated their lives to the service of the gospel message could fail so drastically in their personal lives. As time has gone on it would appear that the percentage of priests who abused children is at least as great as the percentage of abusers in the general population, in so far as that can be judged. One would have thought that it should be much less, given that priests were presented as people whose lives were dedicated primarily to following the teachings of Jesus. As a consequence of the whole sorry debacle, two issues came into sharp focus: the nature of priesthood and the sexual teaching of the Catholic Church.

7

The Roots of the Problem

*T*his chapter is an attempt to delve into what I consider are some of the factors that contributed to the problem of clerical sexual abuse, and might explain why so many priests and religious sexually abused children. Again, in the interest of fairness, it must be acknowledged that the large majority of priests and religious did not abuse children.

I was impressed by a quote from Cardinal Oswald Gracias of India, who is one of the council of cardinals advising Pope Francis. He was speaking in advance of a meeting of the presidents of all episcopal conferences around the world, called by Pope Francis to discuss the sexual abuse scandal within the Church. Gracias said that he hoped the meeting would go beyond strategies of abuse prevention (i.e. structures and guidelines) to considering the root causes underlying why some clergy have harmed children. 'What is the reason why this happened? What is the cause? That's what I would be most concerned about. The whole mentality, the whole culture, we must tackle the problem by the roots.'

From what I read of that meeting I don't think Gracias got his wish. The meeting didn't delve into the roots of the problem in any serious ways. Despite Pope Francis' efforts to promote open and free discussion, synodality as he calls it, we are still a long way from official

Church gatherings being capable of looking seriously at traditional Church teachings. It is striking that such teachings are discussed freely by many people but any debate on the matter seems to be beyond the capability of episcopal conferences.

What are the roots? In seeking an answer, I think we need to look closely at two of the long-established teachings of the Church on priesthood and sexual morality. When one begins to question Church doctrine one is on dangerous ground, but that is part of the freedom I have had since I was suspended from public ministry by the Redemptorists under orders from the Vatican. 'Freedom's just another word for nothing left to lose', as the song says, and I am in the happy position that, in this aspect of my life, I have nothing left to lose.

I'll start with the teaching on priesthood. Pope Francis regularly and consistently attacks 'clericalism', by which I presume is meant a sense of being part of a privileged elite with special powers and status. The problem is that clericalism is, I believe, an inevitable consequence of the doctrine of priesthood. Church teaching tells us that when a man is ordained to the priesthood he undergoes a change, and that from then on he is acting 'in persona Christi', in the person of Christ, and he assumes the position of being 'a mediator between humans and God'. The theological phrase that is used to describe this doctrine says that a man is 'ontologically changed' at ordination, meaning, in so far as I understand it, that he is changed at some fundamental level of his being, of his person. By any standard, this is a fairly perilous teaching, which will have to be abolished if we are to rid the Church of clericalism. It is a teaching that elevates an ordinary man into a position of status and power, a power that is upheld as based not on any particular talent or achievement of his own, or of any human institution, but one coming from God. To act in the person of Christ is an immense concept, and it is no wonder that this understanding of priesthood has, according to many commentators, attracted men who like to wield power, and who see themselves as not being subject to human scrutiny, because their position of power comes from God. I have witnessed many examples of it in my time as a priest. Bishop Long of Australia sums it up very well, and dates its origins back to the early centuries:

The culture of clerical hegemony has been solidly entrenched in the Catholic Church ever since it took centre stage in the Roman Empire. It is a by-product of the model of Church, which sees itself as self-sufficient, superior to and separate from the outside world. Its security, reputation and internal relationships are the centre of attention. The Church in this model becomes the Church of the ordained at the expense of the baptised.

From what I have read it seems that most of the experts say that sexual violence and sexual abuse of various kinds have more to do with the exercise of power than with sexual attractiveness. The fact that priests were invested with power by virtue of ordination and the fact that people were very slow to question this power were contributory factors to clerical child sexual abuse.

My general impression is that the Australian Church has squared up to this problem more honestly than other countries, including Ireland. The report of the Royal Commission into Institutional Responses to Child Sexual Abuse was critical of priestly celibacy and the Church's pessimistic view of human sexuality. Another voice from 'down under' focused on the difficulties surrounding the notion that ordination sets priests apart from the rest of the community. Geraldine Taylor Robinson, speaking to the convention of the Australian Council of Priests in September 2018, and also quoting from Irish author Marie Keenan, had this to say on the topic:

By and large our understanding of the priesthood has been influenced by particular theologies that have seen priesthood as a personal gift or calling that elevates the man above the laity. As Marie Keenan so accurately observed:

'Influenced by this theology of priesthood, it is little wonder that priesthood was construed by clergy and laity alike as a personal gift and a permanent sacred calling, rather than a gift of service to the community. It is also little wonder that a corrosive culture of clericalism was to be born from such a theology, which was to affect clergy and laity alike.'

It is a reality that in our church at the current time, we still have senior hierarchical figures that are proposing and promoting a theology of ontological change at ordination which elevates ordinary men and distinguishes them from lay men. I propose that this is unhealthy. This theology appeals particularly to young men who have a rigid cognitive style, an unintegrated sexuality, and an unconscious sense of powerlessness that they seek to counter with the trappings and power that is afforded them by the church hierarchy and the laity at ordination.

For me, one of the key phrases here is 'an unconscious sense of power-lessness'. Young men with low self-esteem and little sense of their own worth are easily drawn to a career that offers the kind of status that priesthood provides and, once getting a taste of this power, can be prone to abusing it. Geraldine Taylor Robinson and Marie Keenan really hit the nail on the head in exposing the roots of the problem of clerical sexual abuse. The theological notion that a person at ordina-tion is 'ontologically changed' is unhealthy and dangerous, and needs to be abolished. While men at ordination still believe in this 'transfor-mation' clericalism will continue to flourish. However, when we see that this understanding of priesthood goes back to the early centuries, we can recognise that it will be very difficult to change. In the present structure of the Church we are a long way from being able to seriously examine something that has been a 'sacred' doctrine and tradition from the early centuries.

Eight years ago, when commenting on one of the reports on clerical child sexual abuse in a diocese in Ireland I wrote the following sentence in an article in the Redemptorist magazine, *Reality*: 'Priesthood as we have it today is certainly not what Jesus intended.' The Vatican was not best pleased with this statement. I think that even the most doctri-naire official of the Congregation for the Doctrine of the Faith could hardly argue with it now. Jesus was clear that those who were to be in authority in the kingdom must be servant of all, and the greatest among us must be the least. The words of Marie Keenan and Geral-dine Taylor Robinson resonate with Jesus' call to his followers to give service. Nowhere do we hear Jesus advising his disciples to make rigid rules for the communities, and to exercise control over them.

Bishop Long, again Australian, also comments on the exclusiveness of the priesthood and the attendant problems when he states:

The ordained becomes an exalted and elitist club that protects the inter-ests and privileges of its members. This explains the obfuscation and cover-up, which is so endemic to this club mentality. It is a far cry from the model of the Humble Servant that Jesus exemplified and this celibate clerical club provides the ideal condition for the disease of clericalism to foster.

Nothing can justify a system that leads people to believe that priesthood gives them power to rule over and dominate people in any way.

Given the model of priesthood that we have had in the Catholic Church, I believe that in order to get to the roots of the problem of clerical sex abuse we need a radical re-imagining of the notion of ministry in the Church. The first essential step is to break the link between celibacy and priesthood. Celibacy can remain an option for those who take on ministerial responsibility, but it should not be an essential requirement. Let those who wish to live a celibate life make a free choice to do so, and do it for its own sake rather than as a prerequisite for ministry of any kind. This breaking of the essential link between celibacy and priesthood is the second necessary change I believe has to be made, and without it we are going nowhere. So, while Pope Francis constantly, and correctly, bewails the evils of clericalism, but does not also raise the question of compulsory celibacy, he is missing out on one of the basic elements of clericalism, as rightly identified by Bishop Long when he refers to the celibate clerical club. I know that 'celibacy for the kingdom' has been a feature of Christian living from the earliest days, and of course in other beliefs and societies going back even further, but I would have to say that, after a life spent in the priesthood, I am not convinced that it is a life-enhancing way for a person to live unless it is freely chosen for its own sake, and not as a condition of priesthood, or indeed of religious life. I am aware that this is a somewhat contentious thing to say, considering the long tradition of religious life, but we now have a much greater understanding of the human person than previous generations, and we know much more about the longings and the deep needs of the human heart. We also know that the repression of sexuality almost inevitably leads to a distortion of a person's humanity and is in danger of breeding warped sexual activity.

A married priesthood would not necessarily solve the problem of the shortage of priests, but it would generally promote a healthier atmosphere in the clerical world. The presence of women, even if only in the role of wives and partners, would help to break the narrow, somewhat claustrophobic world of priesthood as it prevails today. Allowing a priest to marry and have children would introduce other voices into his life – voices that might challenge the dogmatism of the Church's official teaching.

The style of seminary training, as it exists today, goes back to the Council of Trent in the sixteenth century. Some efforts have been made in recent years to update and modernise the training of priests. Numbers, of course, are much smaller, and here in Ireland we have only one diocesan seminary, whereas 50 years ago we had at least seven, as well as numerous novitiates and seminaries training prospective religious priests. In retrospect, it is questionable if we can view those times as indications of a healthy society. The system within seminaries is still essentially the same, separating candidates for priesthood from the broader society, causing the trainee to see himself as distinct from the wider community, making it difficult for him to interact with people as an equal pilgrim on the journey of life. It needs to be radically overhauled, with preparation for priesthood conducted much more within an apostolic and community setting. Knowledge is important, and academic qualifications will continue to be a significant part of preparation for priesthood, but it must be done in a much more open and natural setting. I am aware that some work is put into preparing young men for celibate living in the modern seminary, with the help of lay experts. However, the question arises as to how this can be done satisfactorily within the seminary setting in which the Catholic teaching on sexuality is upheld – a teaching that declares all forms of physical sexual expression outside of marriage to be gravely sinful, and where same-sex attraction is categorised as a disordered state. Students in the seminary are strongly discouraged from having any close relationships involving sexual expression so that any such association has to be furtive. I fail to see how growth into emotional and sexual maturity can happen in such circumstances.

A truly important step in redesigning priesthood/ministry in the Church is to return to the practice of the early Church. The priest should emerge from the Christian community in which she or he will serve, and be chosen, at least in part, by that community. In this way the person ministering to the community is also an integral part of that community, and I believe that there will be a much better chance that that person will recognise their role as servant of the community, rather than someone who lords it over them. Our present system assumes that priesthood is a full-time occupation. If we allow for a married clergy, and if the priest is drawn from the community of believers, there is no reason why the priest would not have another ordinary occupation – factory worker, postal worker, medic. Such a development would mean that the role of the priest would be pared back to the essentials – presiding at the Eucharist, administration of sacraments. The training would have to adapt to this reality – block courses in theology, placements with other priests, emphasis on delegation and team ministry. The present system of the full-time celibate priest would continue for those who freely choose that life, and the part-time and full-time priests could work together in a team ministry, also involving lay parishioners. This idea has been strongly promoted by German Bishop Fritz Lobinger, who has written extensively on this model.

Another very effective way to eradicate the damaging effects of clericalism would be to allow for a form of priesthood that would be time limited. In other words, that somebody could serve as a priest for five years, ten years or whatever, and when the term was completed they would cease to exercise ministry as a priest. Even better, they could cease being a priest, having, in the best sense of that phrase, done their time, and made their contribution to the community. I know this suggestion cuts across a very basic understanding of priesthood in the Church, that a man, from once he is ordained, remains a priest for ever. At ordination we were told, using the sentence from the Old Testament, 'You are a priest forever, according to the order of Melchisedech.' However, I do think that the idea of a limited term of priesthood is more in tune with the constantly changing reality of the modern world, and the fact that more people are attuned to changing their profession or occupation at different stages in their lives. Such a move would also help to demystify the priesthood and lessen the demarcation between the priesthood and the lay state.

In order for all this to happen, Church authorities, especially those in the Vatican, would need to recognise and accept that Jesus did not ordain the apostles at the Last Supper, and that, in fact, he did not ordain anyone. This is widely acknowledged by Scripture scholars. For example, in a recent letter to *The Tablet* magazine, which deserves to be quoted in full, Irish Augustinian Dr Kieran J. O'Mahony OSA, reflecting on Pope Francis' response to the Amazonian Synod, and his decision not to approve of the ordination of married men, or women deacons, writes:

Has the Holy Father made a mistake in not permitting the ordination of women, even initially only to the diaconate? The exclusion of women from ministry can be traced not only to tradition but also to an erroneous reading of the evolution of 'church' and its ministries.

In common with many other biblical scholars, I would affirm the following. Firstly, the historical Jesus encountered very few non-Jews. His ministry was 'to the lost sheep of the house of Israel'. Jesus did not foresee a separate religious movement, later given the name Christianity.

Much less did he foresee a Church (the term is found in Matthew's Gospel alone), with specific structures and ministries. In the New Testament, varieties of ministries are indeed evident, in particular in Paul, Matthew and Luke-Acts. Towards the end of the first century, these settled into servants, elders and overseers (the later deacons, priests and bishops). The Council of Trent, in affirming that all seven sacraments were somehow instituted by Jesus, made the mistake of accepting the way the Reformers posed the question. This was unnecessary (though understandable in pre-critical times) and brings with it insurmountable historical difficulties.

If the above is substantially accurate, then the historical Jesus 'ordained' nobody at all and the Last Supper was not an ordination service, simply because the historical Jesus did not reckon with a body separate from his own Jewish faith.

As a result, the argument from the Last Supper that only men can be ordained makes no sense. What we have inherited, across the Christian centuries, is the Spirit-guided tradition, reflecting a graced evolution. There is no reason to think that the Holy Spirit has stopped guiding us in these critical times. Listen to what the Spirit is saying to the Churches!

As an aside, when I read this letter, I realised how much has changed in the past ten years, in that a Scripture scholar can say, with such certainty, without fear of any repercussions, that Jesus did not ordain anybody. Not only is he saying that Jesus did not ordain anybody, but that he did not found a church, or at least not one similar to what we have at present. For me, that is good news.

Unfortunately these ideas have never been filtered down to the ordinary believers because Church leaders have not come to grips with an educated laity. Historically, Jesus was a Jew, so his concept of priesthood would have been the priests in the Temple in Jerusalem. We know that he didn't have a high regard for them, and that they were largely instrumental in having him put to death. The Eucharist has its origin in the Last Supper but priesthood certainly does not. It developed only gradually in the early Church over the first 150 years or so, and has gone through many changes down through the centuries.

Is this important? It is, because as long as the magisterium of the Church holds that priesthood as we have it today has come directly from Jesus, they will use that as their argument that nothing can change. As a result, while this remains the official position, the freedom to rethink this ministry in a way that will be more suited to the needs of today's circumstances will continue to be blocked by the Church magisterium.

Another practice of the early Church, indeed of the Church up to relatively recent times, was allowing the believing community to have some say over who should be appointed as their bishop. The present system, where the Vatican makes the appointment, with a minimum of secretive consultation by the papal nuncio to the country, has shown itself to be very inadequate, as well as insulting believers by treating them like children. At this stage most people accept that the Church is facing a major crisis, probably on the scale of the Reformation in the sixteenth century, if not an even greater upheaval. The greatest need for any institution facing such a challenge is good leadership, and there is a dearth of this in the Church, both in Ireland and internationally, at present. A time of crisis needs people with a breadth of vision, the courage to proclaim it, and the ability to excite people and get them to buy into the vision. Our Church is not short of such people. But the structures of leadership are so controlled and exclusive, that at present these voices are not being heard.

The changes to priesthood outlined in this chapter would not have prevented clerical child sexual abuse but they might have lessened the extent of it, recognised the damage it causes to those on whom it is visited, and dealt with it more effectively and honestly.

It is my belief that there are facets of Catholic sexual teaching that have contributed to the incidents of clerical sexual abuse. One of the biggest problems with Catholic teaching, dating back to the early centuries, is its negativity towards any form of sexual expression. Particularly from the time of Augustine sexual relationships were seen as a necessary evil; necessary for the propagation of the species, but to be limited as far as the dictates of the Church could make them, to that sole purpose. This severe constraint was imposed by categorising every sexual thought or action as a mortal sin. Sex was only permissible in marriage for the purpose of procreation, and outside of marriage even a sexual thought, and all sexual actions, either with oneself or with others, were considered to be in the most serious category of sin. If ever there was a negative message that was it. People suffered greatly as a result of this teaching. We now know from psychology what a fundamental part sexual identity plays in the make-up of a person, and how deep the desire and longing for intimacy is ingrained in each of us, but human nature has not changed and people always knew this instinctively. Surrounding sexuality, and its expression, with such a negative message surely had repercussions on people's emotional welfare. Add to all of that the edict that the priest must observe lifelong celibacy, deprived of any sexual expression, any physical intimacy, and you had a cocktail that could give rise to suppression, even repression, of an important part of selfhood. When any possibility of sexual expression is completely repressed, it can manifest itself in warped and destructive ways, and one of these detrimental ways is likely to be clerical child sexual abuse. I know that the counterargument to this theory is the fact that the great majority of child sexual abuse occurs within families and is perpetrated by people who are married or engaged in overt sexual relationships. It is also true that many, many priests and religious who are deemed to be celibate have not sexually abused minors. I cannot argue with this fact but that does not, in my opinion, devalue my belief that the combination of enforced celibacy and negative teaching around sexuality is linked to clerical child sexual abuse.

I know from my long years in the priesthood, from talking to priests, that many struggled with their sexual desires. It is only natural that they would. In itself it should not have been a matter for any great concern, just an indication of the humanity of the person – unless you believed that every sexual thought, every act of masturbation, was a mortal sin punishable with hell. This leads on to the inevitable belief that you are in a more-or-less constant state of sin and ultimately a bad person. In other words, your self-image, your belief in your own goodness and worth, is irreparably damaged. This self-rejection becomes an obstacle to growth and maturity as a person, and leaves the person stunted and failing to reach their potential. That of course is a tragedy in itself, and also for the person's ministry as a priest, except for the fact that many priests had enough common sense and enough faith in themselves to disregard the letter of the law. Some of them also were lucky enough to be in a close, intimate relationship with another person – either male or female – but that has always been kept 'quiet' in the Church. After all, how could a person who has been ontologically changed have the normal sexual desires of the rest of humanity? However, a person in a state of stunted growth, who was not sexually integrated, would be in greater danger of veering off into inappropriate and damaging forms of behaviour. We know that addictions of various types were common enough among priests, maybe especially an addiction to alcohol. Sitting at home in empty presbyteries at night, with no companion to share their lives, and feeling lonely and depressed, is it any wonder that some men had recourse to forms of escape? Maybe it is not that surprising that some of these men ended up in abusive sexual situations, and as altar boys were the most accessible, more often than not young boys became the target.

Some people, including commentators with a particular agenda, have observed that many victims of clerical sexual abuse were young boys and used this as evidence to say that the abusers were largely homosexual, and that gay priests were mainly to blame for what happened. This shows a total lack of understanding of the homosexual orientation and is discriminatory against a cohort of people. It is as if those who make such a suggestion cannot comprehend that gay people are as capable of having as healthy an attitude to their sexuality as heterosexual people and can engage in warm, nurturing adult sexual relationships. Whatever experience I have gained over the years would suggest that responsibility for clerical child sexual abuse cannot be laid at the door of the gay community. Young altar servers, who were around sacristies and in and out of priests' houses, were easy sexual prey for someone who was frustrated, unhappy, disturbed and possibly addicted to dysfunctional sexual expression.

Forming a mature relationship of closeness and equality with a woman was a difficult task for a priest, though a great many have attempted it at some stage in their lives. Many of those eventually left the priesthood and got married. Others couldn't cope with their feelings of guilt and usually ended the relationship abruptly and without giving much thought to the effects on the woman. Church authorities took a much more serious view of a priest having an adult relationship with a woman, especially if the bond was one that seemed to have some depth and seriousness to it, than they did of the other more perverse forms of sexual expression. This skewed perspective could be due to a fear that a priest who was in a relationship with a woman was 'losing his vocation', letting go of the ontological change that he underwent at ordination.

Child sexual abuse was seen as a sinful action that could be dealt with in confession, and wasn't ultimately a danger to his vocation.

In spite of the narrow emphasis on sexuality that pervades a celibate priesthood, I know that there are some priests who have managed to develop strong, mature relationships with women, based on equality and mutual respect. These men have struggled with it, have made mistakes along the way and needed to have confidence in their own conscientious decisions as to what was appropriate in the relationship, and what was for the best for both parties involved.

I know that many other people have written about clerical sex abuse, and have given different interpretations as to why it happened. Whatever the causes, it has to be accepted that the prevalence of abuse among priests and religious is very disappointing. If I am to be consistent in my view that the notion of ontological change is spurious, then I should not be surprised to find that priests are just as likely to be sexual abusers as the population at large. I believe that much of the anger from the laity, when the extent of clerical child sexual abuse was revealed, came from their experience in the confession box. Many had not experienced compassion and mercy when they confessed to using artificial contraception and they now had to stomach the fact that the Church, which had held the line on *Humanae Vitae*, had covered up horrible crimes against children.

Leading on from any mention of the confession box there is now a final question to be posed: what effect will this crisis have on the sacrament of reconciliation/confession? Following on from the Murphy and Ryan reports, some concerns were raised about the seal of confession, something that has been held sacred in Catholic teaching where there is a very strict law that a priest should never reveal what he heard in confession. The question of the confessional seal came up in the context of mandatory reporting, which obliged anyone who received any report of child sexual abuse to inform the police. While some politicians suggested that this applied to the confession box the issue was never seriously examined in this country. On the other hand, the Australian Royal Commission, set up to examine institutional response to child sexual abuse, raised serious questions about the secrecy of confession, and called for legal requirements forcing priests to reveal any such information, no matter the context in which they heard it, including confession. Over the past few years I have given a lot of thought to the subject, having been asked for my views by various media outlets.

Initially, I was inclined to hold to the official Church line that the seal of confession cannot be broken. I questioned how you could make an exception for this particular crime/sin, and not for others. What about the sin of murder, grave theft, even tax evasion? Also, I believed that if an abuser knew that there was a danger that his sin would be reported by the confessor, he would be most unlikely to mention it. Then there were the practical questions – would the priest have to come outside the confession box, ask the penitent for his or her name and address and, if he did so, what kind of reception would he get? Over the years I have heard countless confessions, but I have no memory of anybody ever mentioning the sexual abuse of a child to me in confession. My memory suggests that most people, when confessing sins of a sexual nature, tended to use generalised or fairly vague terms, and this is understandable, given the level of guilt that the Church instilled on the subject of sex of any kind. I had a habit of not questioning people about the details, beyond maybe on occasion asking quietly if they wished to say anything further. Invariably they didn't, and I was happy to leave it at that. A previous generation of Redemptorists were known for questioning penitents closely in this area, and I think my generation reacted against that.

Now when I look at the recommendation of the Australian Royal Commission, I am not as definite in my view that the seal of confession is inviolable in all cases and in all situations. Furthermore, the practice of individual confession has declined greatly. That may not be a bad thing because it was largely associated with precision about the number and times of sins. Then there was the whole business of what constituted a 'good confession', a standard that demanded a 'firm purpose of amendment' without any allowance for human frailty – we do not easily cast off our shortcomings. Most significantly, there was a lack of balance in the celebration, with much more weight given to 'telling the sins' at the expense of any great emphasis on the mercy and compassion of a loving God. There was little recognition that we are saved by love, the love of a God who is at one with the universe, with all of us. I think the best solution now is for the Church to put its emphasis on a more general form of celebrating the sacrament that does not include individual recitation of sins, and includes a general absolution. With the waning of individual confession there is an opportunity for the Catholic Church to change the form of the sacrament and this should start when children are preparing to receive the sacrament for the first time. The single person going into a confession box could be gradually phased out, while priests would still be available to people who wished to come for advice or help with various issues in their lives. The advantage of this would be that the Church, rather than giving way on the seal of confession, would be able to circumvent the issue with general forms of confession. The real travesty would be to allow child sexual abusers to believe that their wrongdoings were absolved without having to accept any responsibility for their actions. In looking at this issue, it is imperative that we do not exclude anyone from God's love. The gospel quotes Jesus as saying that it was better for anyone who offends against children to be cast into the depths of the sea but there is no evidence that he excluded anyone from the all-encompassing love of the Father.

Very few, if any, problems can be traced to a single cause. The root of any single incident of sexual abuse has many possible causes – some located in the individual abuser, some originating in society and the wider culture. Our model of priesthood and Catholic sexual teaching cannot be said to account for all child sexual abuse but, in my opinion, they were certainly contributing factors.

8

Mass Requires Community Participation

Now that I am no longer celebrating Mass in a public setting, and only occasionally doing so in a small group or with one or two other people, I mostly experience Mass as a member of the congregation, down in the pews. It strikes me that I should have done more of that during my years of ministry, because it is certainly, for a priest, a learning experience. To be truthful, attending Mass from the pews is often not a very nourishing experience for me. I know that this is most likely my problem and is linked with my own personal experience. The ambivalence that now defines my relationship with Church and priesthood comes between me and what is happening in the sanctuary, and I have to accept that they are my own issues.

I know a great many people are having difficulty with the latest translation of the text of the Mass, imposed on us by the Congregation for Liturgy a couple of years ago. By any standards it is quite appalling; stilted, artificial language constructed in such a way as to hide, rather than illustrate, the meaning that is intended to be conveyed, and it is also, in many instances, really bad theology. But I have learned that the person in the pew can often get into a semi-dreamlike state where the words pass over one's head, without much attention being paid to them. In this way it is sometimes possible to get through the Mass without being annoyed or irritated by the language – that's on a good day. It is when I begin to think about how this translation came to be imposed on the Church that I get angry, so it is best for me that I do not dwell too much on the manner in which it was foisted on the Catholic community. Feelings of anger are not compatible with participation in the Eucharist. Any possibility of getting some spiritual nourishment out of the event is greatly lessened. The original translation from Latin of the words of the Mass after the Second Vatican Council was done in haste and, in fairness, the people working on it at the time realised this. In the late 1970s, under Pope Paul VI, a commission was set up, the International Commission for English in the Liturgy, now referred to by the acronym ICEL, for the purpose of producing a new translation. It was representative of a wide cross-section of liturgical and linguistic experts and this group were ready to present a new translation in 1998. The people in the Vatican cancelled the years of work that had been done by ICEL and set up a new group, Vox Clara, who were charged with producing a translation that was as close as possible to the text of the Latin Mass. The motivation for this action was ideological, not spiritual, to satisfy a small but powerful group who wanted rigidity and uniformity in the Sunday liturgy. There was no concern for the people attending the Mass. It was a shameful act of betrayal of the Catholic celebration of the Eucharist. There was little or no attention given to the needs of the community whose members are at the heart of the Eucharist. The people in authority at the Vatican at the time, mainly Pope John Paul II and Joseph Ratzinger, later Pope Benedict, were complicit in this betrayal. The current translation, in my opinion, has done enormous damage to the Church. Apart from the awkward language, the theology underlying many of the prayers is a reversal to a way of thinking that is more suited to the nineteenth than the twenty-first century. I have already dealt with issues around the Creed, and the image of God portrayed there. I have written about the belief that Jesus came to appease the anger of God and open the gates of heaven, and I have suggested that this concept no longer makes sense, given our modern understanding of creation and humanity, and of the Divine. However, the current text of the Mass has amplified an old theology that no longer makes sense to the majority of the believing community.

In my opinion, there is another problem, just as fundamental as the ones mentioned above – the idea that body and soul are entirely separate units within the human person, which portrays the person as divided. For the longest period of the Church's history, dating back to at least the fourth and fifth centuries, there was a belief in Christian theology that the person was divided into two separate entities, a body and a soul. Of these two, the soul was viewed as the really important one and the body was seen as having much less significance. As time went on this belief solidified into the notion that there was conflict between these two entities, the soul being the seat of goodness and the body the seat of sin and evil. This perceived dichotomy often finds expression in the phrase 'the weakness of the flesh'. In parallel with this belief, it was also accepted that our only real purpose in this life was to save our souls, to get to heaven. Life was portrayed as a battle between these two entities, the soul and the body, representing good and evil. The body was the enemy; its passions and desires were the gateway to sin and eternal damnation. In popular preaching this battle was often compared to the mythical battle in heaven between the good and bad angels, and this belief about the nature of the human person developed into a dominant anti-body spirituality. It put a major emphasis on self-abnegation, denying oneself, punishing the body, which in religious life sometimes bordered on masochism. Fasting, sometimes to an excessive degree, and various other forms of physical deprivation were promoted. Most of these are not bad in themselves, as long as they are practised in moderation. Nowadays, in the secular world, many of the same things are being encouraged, in the interests of good health, long life and attractive appearance. It is significant to note how very often these practices can be pushed to extremes – the same attitudes but motivated by different beliefs, the zeal for religious fervour versus the fanaticism with appearance or physical fitness.

What was really damaging about the Church teaching was that it sanctioned a rejection of, and unease about, the body. This led to a divided personality which was harmful in so many ways, especially to the psychological welfare of the person who often did not experience a sense of unity and wholeness. Anything to do with bodily pleasure became highly suspect and generated unhealthy guilt feelings. In recent years the Church had begun to move away from that kind of thinking, but the current text of the Mass summons up this dualistic notion of the person once again. At the beginning of Mass, the priest greets the people with 'The Lord be with you', and, in the past, we replied simply 'And also with you'. But now we are instructed to reply 'And with your spirit'. Why only his spirit? It is clearly harking back to the traditional notion that only the spirit matters; the body is of no importance. Before we receive communion we used to say 'Say but the word and I will be healed'. Now we are told to say 'Say but the word and my soul shall be healed'. Again, here we are emphasising the split in the person. Some people might regard things like this as of little or no importance. But I see it as the Church authorities using the Mass text as a means of trying to restore old ways of thinking, old understanding of the divine presence, of the human person and of salvation. It is surely not right or just to use the Mass in such a way. The understanding of God that I am seeking to present is that of the Divine, fully present in the totality of the human person, spirit and body, without any division between the two. They are intrinsically bound together and constitute the fullness of humanity in each of us. We are made in the image and likeness of a God who is one, we are called to union within ourselves and to union with God, and this means that body and soul are one. So, to ask that our souls would be healed without that healing embracing the whole human person makes no sense.

I am well aware that it could be said that the issues I have raised are somewhat pernickety, considering the significance of what is happening at a Mass, and I accept that. When I am attending Mass, I endeavour to shut out these questions and doubts and to concentrate on the fundamental reality. However, there is one part of the text that I struggle with more than any other – when I am paying attention and if my mind has not wandered – it's as if my antenna is finely tuned when it comes to the words of consecration. When the priest is praying over the chalice, speaking the words that are attributed to Jesus at the Last Supper about the shedding of his blood, the older text said 'It will be shed for you and for all', but now, according to the new text, the words ascribed to Jesus state 'It will be shed for you and for many'. As I say, if I am still tuned in at that stage I wonder who exactly is being excluded with the word 'many'. Why is it not for 'all' any more? I have read the various justifications for using that word, but none of them make sense to me, for example that 'many' is a precise translation of the Latin word 'multos'. To this I answer, the language used by Jesus at the Last Supper was Aramaic, not Latin. I think of how Jesus made a point of mixing with the outcasts and the poor, the pariahs of society. The message he came with, the good news of the Kingdom of God, was clearly meant for everyone. So why, at the most sacred moment of our Mass, do we introduce an excluding word, 'many', rather than the inclusive word 'all'? It strikes an unnecessarily jarring note, and it always throws me when I hear it.

Those of my generation clearly remember a time when all Catholic churches around Ireland were packed each weekend for Mass. It is hard to be sure what measure of faith that denoted. To say that those were halcyon days for the Church would be putting a somewhat doubtful interpretation on what was happening. There were two very strong influences at work. Firstly, Church teaching stated that deliberately missing Mass at the weekend was a mortal sin, punishable by eternal damnation. Secondly, social pressure was a substantial factor, to such an extent that someone who was not a regular Mass attendee stood out, and could be subjected to a degree of discrimination in various aspects of life. But that has all changed. Now the situation is very different. Numbers attending Mass have declined dramatically, and the people who are present are mostly of the older category. Usually the priest or priests on the altar are also old, more often than not past retirement age. In my experience there is often a heavy, somewhat cheerless atmosphere around the place, which makes it harder to have the type of joyous celebration that befits what we see as the meaning of the Mass. Expecting younger people to attend in any sort of large numbers is probably unrealistic. A further issue is the failure of churches to spend money on liturgy – seldom employing music directors or people versed in liturgy. I am constantly struck by the financial outlay on child protection (at a time when fewer children participate in church activities) compared with what is spent on providing a meaningful liturgical celebration.

I am aware that there is another way of looking at a decision to attend Mass or stay away. It could be viewed that we go to Mass, not to 'get something out of it', but rather to praise God, the source of life, the guiding hand of our universe. This perspective has a validity that does not sit well with a culture that is centred on the self, on the 'What's in it for me?' attitude.

Going hand in hand with the decline in Mass attendance is the even more rapid fall-off in priest numbers, something that will become more pronounced and drastic over the next ten years. All this causes us to wonder what the future holds for church-going and Mass attendance in Ireland. Will we see our churches empty, as happened in parts of the continent? Or can the Irish Church find some dynamic that will bring about dramatic change and revive its fortunes?

When people stop attending Mass, a great many of them lose all contact with the Church or its ceremonies, apart from the occasional baptism, wedding or funeral. The all-pervasive consumer society, driven by nomadic desire (always wanting to have something more and newer), is very powerful, and can easily absorb a person totally, and blot out any possibility of openness to the spiritual dimension of life, openness to God. It is imperative to realise that this doesn't by any means happen to everyone who leaves the Church. Many of those who walk away do so with great reluctance, having made every attempt to hang on by their fingertips. Some are people whose faith is deep, and whose spiritual life is strong, who have a keen awareness of our dependence on a power outside of ourselves, who have a sense of global responsibility for the whole human family. These people now look elsewhere for nourishment and for support. Some go to other Christian denominations; some go to other religions, such as Buddhism or Islam. In the context of what I said about the mystery of God going way beyond all faiths and nations perhaps this is not important. There are those who, while remaining within the Catholic fold, look outside the formal Church structure for a supportive group. I met many of these groups in my travels in the United States, and there is a growing number of such clusters in Ireland. Some just gather to reflect on the Scriptures and to pray together. Others celebrate Mass together. They may have a priest who has departed the formal ministry and who presides at their gatherings, but increasingly they don't feel the need for that any more. In reverting to the practice in the early Church, one of their number who is not an ordained minister presides. They believe that there is no need for a priest, because at baptism we all became part of the priestly people of God. They give expression to this conviction by sharing equally in the Mass. They no longer believe in the necessity of an ordained priest for a celebration of the Mass.

As I write this I have recently read the document written by Pope Francis in response to the Amazonian Synod, when the bishops of that region of South America, where there is a great shortage of priests, asked for permission to ordain some older married men, so that they could celebrate Mass for their communities. Pope Francis has declined to give permission. In his document he states the following: 'The exclusive character in Holy Orders qualifies the priest alone to preside at the Eucharist. That is his particular, principal and non-delegatable function'.

Much as I admire our present pope, this statement does not make sense to me. It does not address the issue of allowing married men to be ordained as priests. If the request of the bishops in the Amazon region was granted, then those married men would be priests and would be 'qualified to preside at the Eucharist'. Some believe that Pope Francis is not willing, on principle, to take this very small step in opening up the priesthood, while others consider that he is just not able to overcome the opposition that he experiences within the Curia.

I recognise that the small groups of believers who are celebrating Eucharist outside of the formal Mass structure are going against the official Church teaching about the Mass. I have a great deal of empathy with them. It is not only in the Amazon region that there is a shortage of priests. Here in Ireland we are staring a similar situation in the face, and it is already present in many parts of Western Europe. Pope Francis' statement comes after he laments the fact that many of the Christian communities in that region have Mass only about once a year, due to the absence of a priest. He says that the Mass is the centre and core of a believing community, yet he refuses to make a necessary change in order to help the situation, even though the bishops of the region have requested him to do so. Instead he falls back on the old mantra that we must pray for vocations, and I find it hard to credit that as an adequate solution. Today's generation of young men do not opt for priesthood as we have it in the Catholic Church. What are people to do? I think there will continue to be a growth in these small groups gathering in halls and houses to celebrate together. In the American Church they are referred to as 'Intentional Eucharist Communities'.

While I fully understand the reasons why people gather in this way, I am not sure that what they are doing is the best way forward. I have attended some of these celebrations, and they certainly have a quality of intimacy, warmth and prayerfulness that is very often lacking in our large churches. Until the Church authorities face up to the problems of a declining priesthood, often there will be no other option. My concern about the Intentional Eucharistic Communities is this. I have always valued the fact that our Church was a large, international, intercultural organisation. There is a paradox in the fact that while the Catholic Church was restrictive in many ways it also opened us up to many different ideas and ways of looking at life and its problems. Having some form of central authority was also helpful, in that it gave us some necessary direction. This central authority has become far too controlling and oppressive, but it does not have to be so. My fear is that small groups can become inward-looking and narrow in their views and attitudes. They can also come to be dominated by one or two strong individuals and, as in that Church to which they are reacting, there can be a democratic deficit. But as long as the Church authorities resist the type of changes necessary to breathe new life into our Masses, small groups are bound to continue and spread. People today don't feel themselves bound by Church laws in the way that previous generations did. They move easily from one religious expression to another, if they do not find nourishment where they are. It is not realistic or credible to continue to claim that our Catholic Eucharist is the only proper one, the only one where the real transformation takes place. The traditional argument for the exclusive nature of the Catholic Mass is that the actions and words of the priest bring about the change in the bread and wine. Since only Catholic priests were held to be validly ordained, only they could bring about this transformation. The argument that was made illustrates the futility of attempting to explain mystery, of trying to reduce our experience of the Divine, of God, to human logic. Church doctrine contended that the 'accident' of the bread and wine remained the same, but the 'essence' was transformed. In other words, the bread and the wine continued to look exactly like bread and wine, but in reality they became something very different, the body and blood of Jesus Christ. It was asserted, and wars were fought over it, that no other Christian denomination had the power to perform that miracle.

Nowadays, many people, including myself, who still believe that Jesus is present in the celebration of the Mass, are not inclined to try to explain it in this or any other fashion, but are happy to leave the 'how' of his presence in the realm of mystery, something to be experienced rather than explained, and we would be very, very slow to say that he is not present in other Christian celebrations. Again, I refer back to my belief that the Spirit of God underlies our whole universe and, if I believe this, the Catholic Mass is only one expression of people's worship of the Divine. I know from my own long experience that something profound and mysterious occurs in the Mass celebration, but to try to explain it is pointless. It is also not helpful to claim that we Catholics are better, holier and contain more of the truth than other Christian or non-Christian denominations. In general I believe that mystery is to be experienced, not understood. It would be much better if all Christian denominations fully respected each other, and stopped claiming that one form of Eucharistic celebration is better than another, or, worse still, claiming that 'Christ is present in our celebration, but not in yours'. I would love to see the day when people would be encouraged to search for the expression of faith that most suits them at the particular time in their life, and that there would be no rivalry between the various Churches, but a recognition that all of them in their own way are channels for the divine presence. The Divine is much greater and more wonderful that any or all of us, and no one Church can claim to own the mystery.

As I write this there is another development happening in relation to the celebration of the Mass, and it is difficult to discern what the long-term implications will be. I am referring to the coronavirus, which has closed our churches and led to a proliferation of online Masses. Most priests and bishops seem to be happy with this as the best alternative available, and we are often told of the large numbers that are joining in online. Two aspects of this development concern me. Firstly, it seems a reversal of the teaching of the Second Vatican Council on the Eucharist, which emphasised the community dimension of the celebration. Observing an online Mass on the screen has much of the characteristics of the pre-conciliar Mass, where the priest, with his back to the people, performed the ceremony, and the people were little more than observers in the seats. Now, on the screen, they are even more observing and distant, while all the action of the ceremony is performed by the priest. To me that is going back to old-style clericalism; the Mass is the possession of the priest.

My second reservation has to do with the main themes of this book. The divine presence is not confined to any particular holy place, symbol or building. It permeates the whole of creation. During the period of lockdown in Ireland we were blessed with lovely spring weather. Nature was at its most vibrant and alive, with beauty bursting out all around us. Why do we have to go to a screen to observe the distant actions of the priest in the church building in order to experience the presence of God? Better to spend this time, a time of a greater degree of quiet and stillness than we would normally experience in the busy rush of our lives, learning to recognise and immerse ourselves in the God within us and all around us. When all this is over, and we can return to our churches to celebrate the Eucharist, we can do so as part of the assembled community, and rather than going to the church building to meet God, we will bring the Divine with us in a deeper way because of all that we have learned in the silence.

9

Can We Say Anything with Conviction about Eternal Life?

No matter how we try to explain the mysteries of life, of creation, we are always facing questions to which we have few, if any, definitive answers. Whether our approach veers towards the traditional interpretation or towards some of the more modern ways of looking at the mystery, we still find ourselves confronted by the inscrutable, the unfathomable, and any response we make has to be tentative. I have suggested that Christian teachers in the past, and some in the present, have tried to describe and explain the Divine, and have presented us with answers to various aspects of existence that are not as convincing today as they may have been in the past. I am referring particularly to major parts of life experience – suffering, evil, death, the possibility of a life after death. In all of these events we encounter the question as to whether or not life has a meaning and, if so, what it might be. These are subjects that have engaged humanity from the beginning, so it would be foolish of me to suggest that I have any more insight into them than the many great minds down through the centuries that have wrestled with these matters. The question I have here is, does an understanding of God, as a presence that is not located in a distant heavenly abode, but rather as a presence that is right here at the heart of continuing creation, shed any new light on these fundamental mysteries?

The traditional Christian explanation of these mysteries went something like this: sin (and, as a consequence, evil) came into the world through the sin of our first parents in the Garden of Eden. This idea is especially present in the writings of St Paul, who went on to say that Christ, through his death, has destroyed sin, and with it death, which is a result of sin. Some scholars say that not all the letters attributed to Paul were actually written by him, and that those that can certainly be ascribed to Paul do not contain this declaration that sin and death came through Adam and were destroyed by Christ. I am not a Scripture scholar and it would be presumptuous of me to get into such a debate. In our faith we have personalised evil, believing there is a principle, or power, of evil that is independent of and outside humanity. This has been called by various names – Lucifer, Satan, the Devil, Beelzebub. Lucifer, we are told, was originally an angel in heaven, but, through pride and a desire for power, he rebelled against God, and in the ensuing battle he and his supporters were defeated by the army of good angels, and he was driven down to hell, where he resides, though he is free to 'wander through the world for the ruin of souls', according to the prayer we used to say at the end of Mass in my young days. The belief is that while Satan is not as powerful as God, he does have power to influence humans and spread evil in the world. As a consequence, within each of us, and also in the world around us, there is a struggle between the power of good and the power of evil, between God and Satan. We are told that in the end good will triumph and evil will be destroyed. We are also told that because Jesus suffered, we too must suffer, but that our suffering can be beneficial and purifying, and if we bear it with patience and perseverance, it will make up for our sins and we will be rewarded in the next life. We are taught that death is the result of sin and, as such, is a punishment, but we can face it with a degree of confidence because the reward of a good life will be great in heaven. However, if we do not live a good life, which in the past was usually measured by the degree to which we kept the Ten Commandments, there is a very different destiny awaiting us. This was traditionally referred to as the Fires of Hell. Some of my ancestors in the Redemptorists became expert at describing this place and its fires with colourful language and gory details. Many people would say that the descriptions of hell owe more to Dante's *Inferno* than to any scriptural text. However, there is a reference to the flames of hell (Hades) in the parable of Lazarus and Dives in Luke's Gospel. The poor man, Dives, is in the bosom of Abraham while Lazarus wants him to come and cool his tongue as he suffers in the flames. It is important to remember that this is a parable – a story that contains a lesson – and, therefore, we must not interpret it literally. One of our great Scripture scholars, Diarmuid Ó Murchú, goes so far as to assert that there is little in the Bible that we can understand literally, that it is largely figurative and imaginative.

If we believe that creation is always happening, that the universe, and everything in it, is in a constant state of evolution, how are we to understand the big questions that surround the notions of sin, death, heaven, hell, eternal life? If we believe that the ultimate purpose energising all creation is divine love, leading everything to the final perfection, where does evil fit in? What about suffering and death?

We are living in a time when death is regarded as the great tragedy, the ultimate defeat, something we must try to avoid and postpone for a long as possible. In the words of Scripture, 'their going looks like a disaster'. In our modern world, the word 'death' is avoided – people no longer die, they 'pass away'. I find it interesting that so many people today, who would insist that they do not believe in a God or a next life, talk about a person 'passing'. I often wonder if they consider the implication of that language. If death means that someone passes, the suggestion is that they are passing to some other place or state, they are going from one place to another. I would have thought that for people who regard this life as all there is, the word 'death' is more appropriate, in that there is a definite ring of finality about it.

Leaving that aside, we are constantly advised, even admonished, in today's society to live our lives in such a way that we can live as long as possible. Medical science is working hard at developing means by which we can prevent ageing, and we are promised that in a short enough time people will live to be well over 100 years of age, and some even suggest that ultimately a time will come when people will not die at all. Humans will live for ever on this earth. But evolution has at its core what Diarmuid Ó Murchú calls a paradox, a process, a cycle of life-death-new life. In other words, without death there could not be new life. This is true, not just of humans, but of the whole of creation. I am writing this in the springtime of Covid-19, when I have more time to observe nature than ever before. The garden where I am cocooning is a constant source of wonder. The blackcurrant bushes are already full of small, green buds, which promise plenty of pots of jam come summer. The apple trees at the bottom of the garden are awash with blossoms, which give hope of a fruitful autumn. All around is fresh and new, which could only come because last year's growth has withered away and died. Life gives way to death, which in turn gives way to new life.

With this understanding, would it be possible for us to lose our dread of death, and instead, at least to some extent, to make friends with it? Death is one of the most fundamental and natural realities that we have to deal with in life, whether it is something that we know is imminent due to illness, old age or any other reason, or maybe just something we know will happen at some time. While we try not to think too much about it, we know that death is inevitable. Shakespeare tells it as it is: 'Thou know'st 'tis common, all that lives must die, passing through nature to eternity'. Death is coming to all of us.

St Paul writes that death is the result of sin, but looking at life from the evolutionary perspective gives us a different understanding. Death is an inevitable, indeed a natural process that happens to every aspect of creation. Even the great stars and planets would appear to have a natural time span. Unless we die new life cannot happen. The Gospel of St John, written around AD 100, tells us that Jesus touched on this idea when he spoke about the grain of wheat; unless the grain of wheat dies, it does not bring forth new life. If we apply this to the human condition we recognise that we must depart in order to clear the space for what is new. Now, in my 70s, I can see this natural process at work. New generations are coming up, with new attitudes, ideas and ways of doing things. Their lives will be very different from mine and they will be different from our generation, culturally, religiously and politically. As it was from the beginning, the world is evolving. The big challenge of ageing is learning to let go, to pass on the baton to those coming after us, hence the importance of retirement. Nature helps us – the natural ageing process means that there are many things we did in our youth that are no longer possible. Our bodies lose their suppleness, their strength and power. We are more prone to sickness and disease. This is all part of nature's way of preparing us to depart this life, making us ready for what Dylan Thomas refers to as the 'dying of the light'. Suffering and sickness, physical and mental decay are also part of this process, and these realities can provide us with an opportunity to exercise acceptance – an acceptance that enables us to allow for the reality of death. I am painfully aware that all this is easier to write about than to put into practice, and I hope and pray that I will be able to accept it all with equanimity when my time comes. To quote from the Buddha: 'Everything is changing. It arises and passes away. The one who realises this is free from sorrow. This is the shining path. To exist is to know suffering. Realise this and be free from suffering. This is the radiant path.'

The belief that the divine presence is at the heart of creation offers me a new perspective on what the mystery of eternity may have in store for us. We will die, but the life-enhancing energy of the Spirit, the fullness of the life to which God calls us and which is within each of us, does not die. This is just another way of speaking about what we traditionally called the soul, but it is different in a very important way. When we talk about eternity we tend to think of ourselves as individuals, we question where we will go, who we might meet again and if we will be the same as we are now in this world. Traditionally, we would refer to the salvation of our souls. However, I believe that, unlike the conventional notion of soul, the Spirit that is in us is not an individual thing. Rather it is the same Divine Spirit that infuses and energises everything, that permeates the cosmos. It cannot die, and consequently neither can we die, in the fullest sense of that word. I believe that in some mysterious way we will be absorbed more fully into the Divine. That spark of the Divine is already in each one of us, it is what unites us with God, with our fellow man and woman, with the whole of humanity, with the entire universe. I believe that eternity is an experience, an awareness, rather than being an exact location. If we think about our present existence, all we are ever sure of is the present moment. Maybe eternity is a series of present moments, moments when we are fully present to the Spirit of God within us. It is my hope that, following our death, we will experience this union with the Divine in all its fullness and thereby enter into a state of peace, a state in which we will cease to 'want' all the things that we keep 'wanting' in this life. Beyond that there is no more I can say and anything I have said has to be very tentative because we are in the realm of mystery. A line from Hopkins resonates: 'I greet him the days I meet him and bless when I understand'. Tim Freke finishes one of his talks with this summary: 'Life is good; death is safe; and nothing matters but love'. It is the love of God that sustains our lives and that is with us in death. This is a great help to us in finding meaning in our lives. If we can develop awareness of the divine presence, the Spirit of God, within us, we have a great bulwark against feelings of aloneness and emptiness. We are not left stranded in this fragile and random world over which we have little or no control. Instead we are part of something greater, more wonderful and enduring, which gives purpose and worth to our individual lives. I go back again to Wordsworth's 'Intimations of Immortality,' which reflects on our journey through the earthly part of our eternal life, the part of it that we live out in this world. We come from a world beyond this one and we come in a state of blessedness, bringing with us a world view that sees everything 'apparelled in celestial light'. As time goes on the world taints us – 'shades of the prison house' begin to close around us as we travel further 'from the east'. We get caught up in temporal business, in the 'inevitable yoke' of earthly matters. However, the poet assures us that we never put aside the innate spark of freedom with which we are born, and I choose this to mean that we are never deserted by our longing for God, the longing and love that brought us forth and which nothing can 'utterly abolish or destroy'. For Wordsworth, we go back to the 'immortal sea that brought us hither'. Maybe it is just the beauty of the language that overwhelms me but this poem speaks to me about eternal life more evocatively than a lot of theology.

We are still left with the problem of evil. It is a reality in the world that we cannot deny. Some of it is outside our control, but a great deal of evil is visited on humanity by ourselves. Each one of us is capable of evil intentions and actions that can hurt and destroy. Where does all that fit in with an eternal life, with the Spirit of God's love within us? I have never found it possible to believe in the existence of hell, as we traditionally understood it, a place of everlasting punishment. I cannot accept that the Divine, who created us in love, and showers us unceasingly with love throughout our lives, could also consign us to a place of eternal banishment and punishment. It would seem to be a total defeat for divine love. If the Spirit of Divine Love is within us, if we share in the divine life, we could not possibly end up separated from the Divine, from God.

Yet there is still the question of evil and how we explain it. Perhaps it is possible that a person would live in such a way as to crush out the divine presence within by becoming consumed with evil, so that when it comes to death, there is nothing of the Divine left; the spark has been totally extinguished, nothing remaining but an empty shell, nothing that can go anywhere. I don't know and I doubt if any other human knows either. If this is so, maybe death is really the end for that person. It is very important that we don't set ourselves up as judges. Another person, regardless of how seemingly evil the life lived, is still 'other', and we do not know what relationship that person has with God.

To finish I go back to Teilhard de Chardin. For him, the universe, guided by the divine presence, is on an evolutionary journey to what he called the Omega Point, the culmination, the completion, which would represent the final triumph of love. If that is the case, and I do believe that it is, who am I or anyone to say that any aspect of this great creative act of the Divine will be lost, to decree that the spark of Divine love has been totally snuffed out in anyone? We fall back on the virtue of hope, as we listen to the words of Jesus from St John's Gospel: 'Let not your hearts be troubled, trust in God and also trust in Me'.

10

Faced with Enormous Challenges, Is There a Future for Our Church?

*I*n this book I have outlined some of the major challenges that I consider the Catholic Church is facing in the immediate and median-term future. There is little enough indication that the Church as it is currently structured has the capacity to tackle some of the more difficult issues successfully. Others are a bit more manageable, and the Church is already making some headway in facing up to them. I am aware that many people, much more qualified than myself, have written extensively on the future of the Church. What I wish to do in this chapter is outline the implications of my views about our faith for our Church; in other words, the type of Church that would, in my opinion, be best suited to promote the message of Jesus of Nazareth to the modern world.

Two interrelated questions must be posed at the beginning of this topic: Did the Church originate with Jesus? Did he found a Church, and, if so, can we say with any degree of certainty that the Catholic Church as we have it today is along the lines of what was in the mind of Jesus?

The gospels tell us that Jesus said to Peter: 'You are Peter, and upon this rock I will build my Church, and the gates of hell shall not prevail against it'. There is no certainty that this sentence can be attributed directly to Jesus. It seems much more likely that it was added some considerable time later by the followers of Jesus. If this is so, it means that it represents the mind of Jesus as interpreted by early followers of Jesus some years after his time on this earth. It is telling us more about the minds of the early believers than giving us a direct account of the words of Jesus. I believe it is an open question whether or not Jesus intended his followers to form themselves into a church institution. When we examine the way he lived his life, and his teaching, it is hard to see much evidence that this was part of his plan. He was clearly the most un-institutional of people. During that period, somewhere between one and three years, of his public ministry, he lived the life of a wandering preacher. His possessions were minimal, and there is no evidence that he attempted to structure any organisation around himself. He gradually became the central figure in a group of followers but it seems to have been more likely that they followed him, having listened to him speak, rather than that he went in search of them. Scripture gives a couple of examples of people whom he specifically invited to follow him, but most just seemed to come along of their own accord. Choosing the twelve apostles may have been some small effort at setting up a structure, but no more than that. It is important to remember that Jesus was born into the Jewish faith and practised the Jewish faith as it was in his time. He attended the synagogue and made his journeys to the Temple in Jerusalem, which were part of the religious practice of the people. He lived and died a Jew, but he never bought into the values or the lifestyle of the contemporary religious institution. In fact he was heavily critical of it, and even of some of its teachings. He railed against the Pharisees, who were the leaders of the local synagogues, using fairly strong language, calling them, for instance, 'whited sepulchres'. He made a vehement and public attack on the priests in the Temple, accusing them of greed and exploitation of the people, and famously seeming to lose his temper, upending tables and scattering money, saying they were turning the Temple into a 'den of thieves'.

Church as institution was not a concept, as far as I know, that was commonly used in the time of Jesus, referring either to the religious structure of the time, or to the buildings in which people gathered to pray. For that reason I find it hard to believe that Jesus of Nazareth would have used that phrase, 'build my church', that is attributed to him. That leaves me with the conclusion that it was Jesus the Christ, in other words the experience that the followers had of him after the resurrection, that may have inspired them to begin to form themselves into some type of institutional structure. As the numbers of followers increased it would have made perfect sense to begin to organise. In every aspect of life it is something that we humans are inclined to do in order to preserve and sustain something that is important to us, something that we want to continue beyond our own earthly existence. However, when the Church teaching proclaims, as a doctrine of our faith, that Jesus founded the Church, this claim cannot be convincingly deduced from that sentence in St Matthew's Gospel, which was addressed primarily to the early Jewish believers. I don't believe that the assertion can convince the modern questioning mind. If we continue to declare categorically that the Church as we have it today takes its origin from Jesus, implying that it is an accurate representation of what Jesus intended, we are on even shakier ground. Down through the centuries the Church has wielded enormous political power, even at times having armies and fighting wars. Today the Church still retains a lot of power, as distinct from influence. It possesses great wealth and grandeur, with its officials wearing the grandest and most ostentatious of vestments, with centralised control and authoritarian structures. Increasingly people find it next to impossible to relate this to the wandering preacher in Galilee 2,000 years ago. This is a real problem, and one that will not easily be solved. How many times have we met people who have gone to Rome, and have visited the Vatican, walked around St Peter's Square, gone into the Basilica and took the guided tour of the Sistine Chapel and the other beautiful works of art? They have been impressed by the grandeur of all that they have seen, but have come home asking what has this to do with the carpenter of Nazareth. I expect that if I had told these people that this is what Jesus had in mind for his Church, they would have laughed me out of court. I think it is fair to say that if Jesus were to return to earth in our time, and knowing what we do about his life and teaching, he would be most unlikely to visit the Vatican, except maybe to do something equivalent to what he did in the Temple – overturning the tables and driving out the money changers. Personally I find it impossible to believe that the Church, as it is now, with its present structure, authority system and long list of rules and exclusions, would be what Jesus might have wished, if indeed he wished for any type of institution at all.

It is widely held that the early believers organised themselves around small groups, usually referred to as house churches, with the head of the house presiding as they followed the example of Jesus at the Last Supper. In time, these came to be known as the Eucharistic gathering. There is reference to these assemblies in the writings of St Paul. As time went on, and the numbers of believers increased, and the message spread to different parts of the Roman Empire, some larger structures inevitably began to emerge. The Acts of the Apostles gives us a rough outline of this transition from discrete groups of believers to a more formal arrangement. The ministry of the diaconate was introduced (and most scholars would also agree that this office was open to both male and female). We get a good insight into these developments in the references to the church at Antioch. We also read of people who were described as *episcopus* and *sacerdos*, words that are usually translated as 'bishop' and 'priest'. There is no certainty about what exactly their function was in the early days, and how it might relate to our present-day bishops and priests, or if these functions were exclusively reserved for men from the beginning. Given the culture of the time it is very possible that the chosen leaders were male, but it is important to recognise that culture changes and that the structures of any group need to reflect this fact if the organisation is to survive.

The Christian faith underwent enormous change in the fourth century. It was then that the much more formal and institutional structure emerged that could probably be said to be more closely related to what we have in today's Church. This was the result of the Roman Emperor Constantine giving freedom of religion to Christians in the early years of that century. By the end of the century, some would say unfortunately, Christianity was the official religion of the Roman Empire. This was the stage at which a structure really developed around this new Christian faith, with styles of organisation and systems of authority and governance. Any institution whose members are spread far and wide, and that is following a particular set of beliefs and teachings, needs some type of organisation and authority system. Can we say with any degree of certainty whether the structure that developed during that century was guided by the inspiration of the risen Jesus, or was merely influenced by the political structure of the Roman Empire? Evidence would seem to indicate that the politics of the day had a regrettably dominant impact on what emerged; in short, the structure of the Church was modelled on the structure of the Roman Empire. The Roman Empire has been gone for about 1,400 years, but the Church retains many of the same systems, and continues to exercise authority in the same centralised and dogmatic fashion, even though society now is dramatically different from what it was at the time of the Romans. The Church appears to pride itself on its reluctance to make any changes. It proclaims that God is 'the same yesterday, today and forever', and asserts that, as a consequence, the Church does not change either.

The Church has, at last, come to terms with evolution, at least most sections of the believing community have. Central to evolution is the notion of change, of fluidity. There is nothing that is fixed and unchanging. The whole of creation is on a spectrum, moving forward, and any person or thing that does not embrace change will find that they are unable to communicate with those who have accepted that life is cyclical – all things go through a process of life, death and rebirth. We live in a constantly changing, mutating reality. Unfortunately we can see plenty of evidence of our Church not being able to come to grips with a changing world. The late Cardinal Martini of Milan was not the only one of us who recognises that the Church is 200 years behind the times. Unfortunately his views on Church stagnation were not made known until after he had died. Perhaps this tells us something about peer pressure within the higher echelons of the Catholic Church.

This brings me to the question of the papacy, which has had a long and chequered history in the Church. The original understanding from the early Church was that the pope was 'the first among equals', in other words he was a bishop, but, as Bishop of Rome, he was a symbol of unity for the whole Church. It was not envisioned that he would rule over other bishops but that he would be a symbol of unity. The power of the papacy gradually increased, reaching a high point during the eleventh and twelfth centuries due to the leadership of Innocent II and Gregory VII. During the Middle Ages the papacy came under the control of some of the powerful Italian families, leading to corruption and scandal on a grand scale. The fact that the papacy governed the Papal States, comprising a large section of what we now know as central Italy, meant that popes were directly involved in the world of politics, with all the power struggles, wars and other conflicts that came with being a ruler of a state. Because of that, for many centuries, the papacy was viewed in terms of its temporal worldly power to the detriment of its spiritual influence. This continued right up to the middle of the nineteenth century, when, with the unification of Italy, the papacy lost the Papal States, and ceased to be a civil and political power. This has to be regarded as a blessing, as it meant that popes had a better chance to focus on their real mission, which was, and is, to promote the message of Jesus of Nazareth. Having lost all political power, the papacy acquired a different sort of power, which was not confined to Italy or Europe, but began increasingly to be felt right around the world. This is usually referred to as 'soft power', meaning the type of influence a person can wield precisely because they have no political or military might behind them. Popes are in a unique position to exercise this type of power. Good examples of it in recent years have been Pope Paul VI's address to the United Nations in 1965 when he made an earnest plea for world peace (that speech was made on the feast of St Francis), the role played by Pope John Paul II in the collapse of communism, his opposition to the United States' invasion of Iraq, and Pope Francis' part in ending the hostility between the United States and Cuba. In the midst of wars and conflicts of various kinds, some popes have been the strongest and most influential voices for peace. From Pope Leo XIII's *Rerum Novarum* in the late nineteenth century to the present time, papal encyclicals have advocated strongly for social justice and care for the poor and deprived. In 1967 Pope Paul VI issued the important *Populorum Progressio*, which advocated that world economics should benefit all people, not just the few. Pope Francis is particularly outspoken in this area. His 2015 document on the environment, *Laudato Si'*, is enormously influential, and has given new energy to the international awareness of the urgency of dealing with climate change. In all of this we can see that the pope is now much more than the leader of the Catholic Church. Depending on the particular person holding the office, he can have considerable influence around the world, where his voice on certain issues carries weight far beyond the Catholic population.

All of this is good, yet there is a negative side to having such a dominant figure as head of the Church. There is no doubt that the notion of a dominant papacy played a significant part in the two major splits that happened historically, the one between the East and the West in the eleventh century and the Protestant Reformation in the sixteenth century. The last half century or so has seen much effort put into ecumenism, attempting to bring the various different Christian

Churches closer together. The reality of a powerful papacy has consistently proved to be an obstacle, because the non-Catholic Christians are reluctant to come under the control of a dominant and powerful papacy. Two developments in the nineteenth century have exacerbated this problem: the declarations of the supremacy and infallibility of the pope. Though the notion of the pope being infallible is the one we tend to hear more about, a declaration that many find difficult to accept, it seems to me that the idea of 'papal primacy' is more troublesome. At least we can say that the exercise of infallibility was fairly tightly curtailed, and has only seldom been brought to bear since it was declared. But the description of the pope as the 'supreme ruler' is a wider and, I believe, more damaging title. He is often referred to as the 'Supreme Pontiff', denoting that he is the final authority, the ultimate ruler.

Pope Francis has been interesting in all of this. When he was elected he immediately referred to himself as 'Bishop of Rome' rather than 'Supreme Pontiff'. This was truly significant. It was a sign that he defined himself, and his role, more in line with the popes of the early Church – first among equals with the other bishops – rather than as the supreme ruler over the other bishops and every other Catholic, which has been the understanding of later centuries. He has followed this up by attempting to decentralise the Church, taking the power away from the Vatican bureaucracy and encouraging bishops to take more responsibility and decision-making at local level, in consultation with the faithful of their diocese, both priests and lay people. It is a radical move, and it remains to be seen how successful it will be. The irony is, that while he is totally sincere in this policy of defining the Church in terms of the community of believers rather than an institution that is solely under papal authority (this policy derives from the teaching of the Second Vatican Council), one of the consequences of his own popularity and increasing influence on the international stage is that a contrary message is, inadvertently, being given. His international stature can cause the Catholic Church to be over-identified with him, and as such can be seen as more Rome-centred than ever. Those of us who are hoping for reform of the Church are tempted to look too much to Francis, and as a result are too inclined to lose hope in him if he does not come up to our expectations. It is risky to make heroes out of people and inevitably leads to disillusionment. It can be cringe-making to hear Francis described as having rock star qualities, because such a portrayal diminishes his ordinary humanity. The decentralisation of the Catholic Church cannot be the work of one man. It requires the input of all believers, clerical and lay. In particular it demands more courage and initiative from the local bishops of each country. To date, the German bishops appear to be the only group in Europe taking up this challenge.

In tackling the reform of Church structures, Francis is trying his best. His vision of a decentralised Church in which more powers of decision-making rest with the regions rather that Rome, of a synodal Church that listens to the voices of the ordinary people, of a compassionate Church that allows for the particular circumstances of the person's life and is less obsessed with laws and rules, seems to be in tune with the life and teaching of Jesus. Francis places special emphasis on the need for the Church to be the Church of the poor, and this is the acid test of all of us in judging our commitment to Christianity. The amount and level of opposition he is meeting, particularly from senior people within the institution, is quite disturbing. I have learned over the years that religious belief, even in its more intense form, is no guarantee of good attitudes or good behaviour. The history of all the major religions illustrates that very clearly. It is also my own personal experience. Over the years I have had many discussions with people of other faiths and with those who have no particular belief in any type of divine presence, and we could respect each other's beliefs without conflict. But in my dealings with some Catholics I have been verbally attacked and abused, judged and condemned, told with total certainty that I was heading for eternal damnation. Religious belief is a heady brew that can easily lead to extremism of various sorts. We are seeing that now in the reaction of some Catholics, some bishops and some cardinals to Pope Francis. It is not a pleasant sight.

So what is the future for our Church? Before we begin to discuss this, we must remember that it is beyond difficult to estimate the extent of the damage done by the revelations of clerical sex abuse and the way it was handled by the authorities. How long will it take the Church to restore its good name and credibility? I expect it will take generations. But its impact goes far deeper than the matter of credibility. The realisation that priests used minors to meet their sexual needs has put the spotlight firmly on the structures and systems of the Church and has led to a demand for a substantial change in the whole way the Church operates. It is not enough to appoint child protection officers, pay financial compensation and continue as usual.

I have suggested already that we need a different style of papacy, a different form of Church governance. The Curia will need to be substantially reformed, if it is at all possible to reorganise a body that is so deeply embedded, has successfully seen off many efforts to change it and has withstood several attempts to reduce its power and status. Ideally there would need to be a complete clean-out of the present system, but such a major blitz is unlikely.

It is of great importance that the choosing of bishops be done differently. One thing that the recent crises in the Church have shown up clearly is the lack of good leadership. The present secretive system of non-consultation has to be replaced by a method that gives a real say to the people and priests of the diocese. Once appointed a bishop should normally remain in his diocese, and the term of office should be for a defined period of time rather than for life. The policy of transferring bishops to other dioceses can lead to ambitious people looking for promotion and can result in a bishop paying more attention to the next vacancy in a diocese that is considered more prestigious than his present post. The Church of the future must, in so far as is possible, be rid of desire for power, promotion and positions of distinction. These features, which have been characteristic of the Church for many centuries, are contrary to the teaching of Jesus, who wanted leaders to be humble, and servants of all, not lording it over anyone. We have had, and continue to have, a great deal of 'lording it over others' in our Church.

Priesthood, too, needs to change. It will be essential that it be open to married people and to women. It will also be important that we return to the practice of the early Church, when the person who presided at the Eucharist was chosen from the local community, and his or her role was clearly seen as one of service. It would greatly help if all the titles in the Church were abolished, no more monsignori, canons, lordships, reverences or even fathers. No more addressing people as 'My Lord', Your Grace', 'Your Reverence'; let people be known by the name by which they were baptised into the Church. Better still if all the garments and other distinctions that go with the titles could also be abolished.

In all of this the laity will have to play a major part. They will have to be assertive, demanding the change that is necessary. A big difficulty here is the traditional way in which our faith was presented in the Church. We were taught that it was a very personal matter. Our aim was to save our souls, and we were instructed to do that by keeping the commandments, attending Mass and the sacraments, and saying our prayers. The Church was considered to be the perfect society, above and beyond criticism. It won't be easy to get people who were trained to be submissive and not to question (publicly anyway) any doctrine or decision to suddenly think in new ways and to become agents for change in the Church. What is happening instead is that people are leaving the Church in droves, especially in the developed world, appalled at the behaviour of some of its senior people. Many of those who are leaving or have left are probably the ones who would have been most likely to give leadership in pushing for change. Many of those who remain are apt to accept what they are told by bishops and priests and/or to devote their attention to their own personal spiritual life, unconcerned about the bigger issues of the universal Church. Change will not come from them. However, there is a cohort of lay people who want a changed Church and who have not walked away – yet. Some of these people often straddle two worlds; they are in the pews at the weekend but are also attending meetings and events organised by Church reform groups. Others are discussing the need for change in quiet conversations with their friends. Many are older people and tend to have one thing in common in that their adult children, whom they raised as Catholics, have lost any connection with the Church – they might attend at Christmas out of some sense of nostalgia. It is questionable if enough lay people who really care for the future of the Church, and have the courage and ability to help bring it about, will stay around long enough to be part of the solution.

Given the decline in the number of priests, the responsibility for the preservation and transmission of the faith will fall to the laity, the people of God. Consequently, the Church will need lay people who are well versed in theology and spirituality, who have a real sense of the divine presence and of our relationship and the relationship of the universe with that presence. The understanding of prayer will need to go beyond that of making personal petitions to a God that is seen as something of a granter of favours. Karl Rahner once remarked that the believer of the future will be a mystic, or not at all.

There is one other change that I believe needs to happen, and it follows directly from what I and others are saying about a new understanding of the Divine. We have taught in the Church for many centuries that we are the one, true Church, and that all other belief systems are in error. We have sent missionaries all over the world to convert the 'pagans' so that their souls would be saved. The ecumenical movement, which flourished for a time after the Second Vatican Council, has tried to change this way of thinking. Unfortunately, under the papacy of the two previous popes efforts at ecumenism have struggled to survive, despite the fact that Pope John Paul II met many times with the leaders of other world religions. This was good, but not enough in itself without acknowledging the validity of all faiths who believe in God. I am suggesting that we must recognise that we in the Catholic Church don't have a monopoly on God or on truth. The Divine Spirit is present to a greater or lesser extent in the whole of creation, including all the various religious beliefs. We must respect this, recognise the goodness and godliness of others, and learn to work together without any sense of wanting to control.

I do have some hope for the future. Despite what I said earlier about not depending too much on Pope Francis, I am impressed by the document he produced in 2019 for reform of the Curia, *Praedicate Evangelium*. It has currently been circulated for discussion to heads of Vatican departments, national bishops' conferences, papal nuncios and others. If this draft, or even some sections of it, were to be implemented, major changes would take place in Church governance. Many of the changes I have suggested would be more likely to happen. I will briefly summarise its main points:

It aims to decentralise decision-making by devolving more power to local bishops. They would have the task of resolving local issues in accordance with local needs. The caveat is that any such resolutions could not contravene Church doctrine or Church unity and there is always the danger that this would be used to avoid making any difficult decisions. On the other hand, local bishops could no longer hide so easily behind the excuse that 'Rome won't allow us.'

The role of the Curia is re-imagined so that it would be at the service of the local bishops rather than controlling them. The Curia is the civil service of the Church, with various departments, referred to as dicasteries or congregations. This document proposes that the heads of some of these departments would be lay people from the different continents. This would get rid of some of the clericalism that bedevils the Church and would emphasise its universal nature. Under present policy, while the heads of the congregations are appointed for a five-year period, this has become meaningless, as most of them are usually reappointed. A great furore ensued when Pope Francis did not reappoint Cardinal Müller as head of the Congregation for the Doctrine of the Faith. Francis envisages this policy of a set time limit becoming standard practice. That would prevent people setting up their own little kingdoms within the system, which has been a feature of the Curia up to now.

Giving further emphasis to the need for the laity to have a far greater say in the governance of the Church, the document proposes that they are given a greater role in advising the pope on the selection of local bishops – in other words, it would no longer be completely the prerogative of the papal nuncio.

I am well aware that in this book I am looking for major change, and outlining a very different type of Church from what we have at present, and I do not believe that it will happen in my lifetime. One thing is certain: the Church of the future will be smaller, and hopefully more faithful to the gospel. This will not be the smaller, purer Church that Pope Benedict wished for, made up of those who reject the relativism of the modern world. Pope Francis has put paid to that idea by his challenge to believers to be in the world, calling on the Church to act as a field hospital for the needy. The future will be a smaller Church because of the drastic impact of all that we are witnessing in the current Church, which has driven so many people to leave the Church and find their spiritual nourishment elsewhere. As it returns more to the message of Jesus of Nazareth, and frees itself from the counter-messages of wealth, power and control, it will again become a beacon of light in the world that will attract people, not because of its status, but because of the love that it shows towards all.

One way or another, there are stormy times ahead for our Church. Many battles will be fought, and there will be deep divisions, and possibly splits and breakaway groups. I like the summary given by American writer Michael Bayer, writing about the radical changes needed in our Church: 'The purgation will hurt. Smashing the patriarchy, extirpating the racism, eliminating the privilege and the self-satisfaction and the moral superiority is going to be painful as hell for a 2000-year-old institution that has accumulated much that has nothing to do with the gospel.'

Epilogue

This is the document that I referred to in my introduction. It came to me, by the usual circuitous route, from the Secretary of the Congregation for the Doctrine of the Faith to the Superior General of the Redemptorists, to the Provincial of the Irish Redemptorists, and then to me. They don't believe in direct communication, or else they don't regard me as being of sufficient significance to be dealt with directly. As I have already stated, I will not, indeed I could not, sign any of these propositions.

1. The Reservation of Priesthood to Men Alone

The following paragraph is taken from the Apostolic Letter, *Ordinatio Sacerdotalis* of Pope John Paul II (1994).

4. Although the teaching that priestly ordination is to be reserved to men alone has been preserved by the constant and universal Tradition of the Church and firmly taught by the Magisterium in its more recent documents, at the present time in some places it is nonetheless considered still open to debate, or the Church's judgment that women are not to be admitted to ordination is considered to have a merely disciplinary force.

Wherefore, in order that all doubt may be removed regarding a matter of great importance, a matter which pertains to the Church's divine constitution itself, in virtue of my ministry of confirming the brethren (cf. Lk 22:32) I declare that the Church has no authority whatsoever to confer priestly ordination on women and that this judgment is to be definitively held by all the Church's faithful.

The following paragraphs are taken from the Post-Synodal Apostolic Exhortation, *Querida Amazonia* (2020). While addressing the strength and gift of women, Pope Francis at the same time affirms the reservation of the sacred priesthood to men alone.

The strength and gift of women

99. In the Amazon region, there are communities that have long preserved and handed on the faith even though no priest has come their way, even for decades. This could happen because of the presence of strong and generous women who, undoubtedly called and prompted by the Holy Spirit, baptized, catechized, prayed and acted as missionaries. For centuries, women have kept the Church alive in those places through their remarkable devotion and deep faith. Some of them, speaking at the Synod, moved us profoundly by their testimony.

100. This summons us to broaden our vision, lest we restrict our understanding of the Church to her functional structures. Such a reductionism would lead us to believe that women would be granted a greater status and participation in the Church only if they were admitted to Holy Orders. But that approach would in fact narrow our vision; it would lead us to clericalize women, diminish the great value of what they have already accomplished, and subtly make their indispensable contribution less effective.

101. Jesus Christ appears as the Spouse of the community that celebrates the Eucharist through the figure of a man who presides as a sign of the one Priest. This dialogue between the Spouse and his Bride, which arises in adoration and sanctifies the community, should not trap us in partial conceptions of power in the Church. The Lord chose to reveal his power and his love through two human faces: the face of his divine Son made man and the face of a creature, a woman, Mary. Women make their contribution to the Church in a way that is properly theirs, by making present the tender strength of Mary, the Mother. As a result, we do not limit ourselves to a functional approach, but enter instead into the inmost structure of the Church. In this way, we will fundamentally realize why, without women, the Church breaks down, and how many communities in the Amazon would have collapsed, had women not been there to sustain them, keep them together and care for them. This shows the kind of power that is typically theirs.

102. We must keep encouraging those simple and straightforward gifts that enabled women in the Amazon region to play so active a role in society, even though communities now face many new and unprecedented threats. The present situation requires us to encourage the emergence of other forms of service and charisms that are proper to women and responsive to the specific needs of the peoples of the Amazon region at this moment in history.

103. In a synodal Church, those women who in fact have a central part to play in Amazonian communities should have access to positions, including ecclesial services, that do not entail Holy Orders and that can better signify the role that is theirs. Here it should be noted that these services entail stability, public recognition and a commission from the bishop. This would also allow women to have a real and effective impact on the organization, the most important decisions and the direction of communities, while continuing to do so in a way that reflects their womanhood.

DOCTRINAL PROPOSITION: *According to the Tradition and the doctrine of the Church incorporated in the Canon Law (c. 1024), a baptized male alone receives sacred ordination validly.*

I, Fr. Tony Flannery C.Ss.R, submit to the above doctrinal proposition given by the Congregation for the Doctrine of the Faith.

Fr. Tony Flannery, C.Ss.R

2. The Moral Liceity of Homosexual Practices

The following paragraph is taken from the Catechism of the Catholic Church n. 2357.

2357. Homosexuality refers to relations between men or between women who experience an exclusive or predominant sexual attraction toward persons of the same sex. It has taken a great variety of forms through the centuries and in different cultures. Its psychological genesis remains largely unexplained. Basing itself Sacred Scripture, which presents homosexual acts as acts of grave depravity, tradition has always declared that "homosexual acts are intrinsically disordered." They are contrary to the natural law. They close the sexual act to the gift of life. They do not proceed from a genuine affective and sexual complementarity. Under no circumstances can they be approved.

DOCTRINAL PROPOSITION: *Since the homosexual practices are contrary to the natural law and do not proceed from a genuine affective and sexual complementarity, they are not approved by the moral teaching of the Catholic Church (cf. CCC 2357).*

I, Fr. Tony Flannery C.Ss.R, submit to the above doctrinal proposition given by the Congregation for the Doctrine of the Faith.

Fr. Tony Flannery, C.Ss.R

3. The Institution of Marriage and Same-Sex Marriages

The following paragraph is taken from the Post-Synodal Apostolic Exhoration *Amoris Laetitia* (2016). In this paragraph Pope Francis affirms that only the exclusive and indissoluble union between a man and a woman benefits society.

52. No one can think that the weakening of the family as that natural society founded on marriage will prove beneficial to society as a whole. The contrary is true: it poses a threat to the mature growth of individuals, the cultivation of community values and the moral progress of cities and countries. There is a failure to realize that only the exclusive and indissoluble union be-tween a man and a woman has a plenary role to play in society as a stable commitment that bears fruit in new life. We need to acknowledge the great variety of family situations that can offer a certain stability, but de facto or same-sex unions for example, may not simply be equated with marriage. No union that is temporary or closed to the transmission of life can ensure the future of society. But nowadays who is making an effort to strengthen marriages, to help married couples overcome their problems, to assist them in the work of raising children and, in general, to encourage the stability of the marriage bond.

The following article is taken from the Catechism of the Catholic Church n. 1660 (cf. GS 48; CIC 1055, §1).

1660. The Marriage covenant, by which a man and a woman form with each other an intimate communion of life and love, has been founded and endowed with its own special laws by the Creator. By its very nature it is ordered to the good of the couple, as well as to the generation and education of children. Christ the Lord raised marriage between the baptized to the dignity of a sacrament.

DOCTRINAL PROPOSITION: *The Marriage covenant, by which a man and a woman form with each other an intimate communion of life and love, has been founded and endowed with its own special laws by the Creator (CCC 1660). Other forms of union do not correspond to God's plan for marriage and family. Therefore, they are not allowed by the Catholic Church.*

I, Fr. Tony Flannery C.Ss.R, submit to the above doctrinal proposition given by the Congregation for the Doctrine of the Faith.

_____

Fr. Tony Flannery, C.Ss.R

4. "Gender Theory"

The following paragraph is taken from the Congregation For Education's document on gender theory in education, "Male and Female He Created Them" (2019).

2. The context in which the mission of education is carried out is characterized by challenges emerging from varying forms of an ideology that is given the general name 'gender theory',

which "denies the difference and reciprocity in nature of a man and a woman and envisages a society with-out sexual differences, thereby eliminating the anthropological basis of the family. This ideology leads to educational programmes and legislative enactments that promote a personal identity and emotional intimacy radically separated from the biological difference between male and female. Consequently, human identity becomes the choice of the individual, one which can also change over time."

DOCTRINAL PROPOSITION: *In so far as it contradicts the foundations of a genuine Christian anthropology, gender theory is not accepted by Catholic teaching* (cf. Congregation for Catholic Education, *Male and Female He Created Them*, nn. 2-4; 19-23 and *passim*).

I, Fr. Tony Flannery C.Ss.R, submit to the above doctrinal proposition given by the Congregation for the Doctrine of the Faith.

_____
Fr. Tony Flannery, C.Ss.R

I, Fr. Tony Flannery C.Ss.R, submit to all of the above doctrinal propositions given by the Congregation for the Doctrine of the Faith as they pertain to the Church's teaching on the: 1. Reservation of the sacred priesthood to men alone; 2. The moral liceity of homosexual practices; 3. The legal recognition of marriage between persons of the same sex; and 4. "Gender Theory."

_____   _____
Fr. Tony Flannery, C.Ss.R.   Date

The document was accompanied by a covering letter from the CDF to the Superior of the Redemptorists. The last paragraph of the letter was as follows:

After the statement is signed and received, a gradual readmission of Fr. Flannery to the exercise of public ministry will be possible by way of an agreement with this Congregation. Furthermore, given the fact that he has stated numerous times that he is not a theologian, he should be asked to not speak publically on the above-mentioned topics which have caused problems in the past.

The letter was signed by Archbishop Giacomo Morandi, Secretary.

Reading List

For anyone who might wish to pursue some of the topics covered in this book, here are some suggestions.

Feehan, John (2018) *God in a Five-Pointed Star: A Spiritual Philosophy of Nature*, Dalgan Park: Columban Ecology Institute.

Lenaers, Roger (2017) *Living in God without God*, Dublin: Carysfort Press.

Mackey, James P. (2006) *Christianity and Creation: The Essence of the Christian Faith, and Its Future among Religions*, New York, NY: Continuum.

Malone, Mary T. (2014) *The Elephant in the Church: A Woman's Tract for Our Times*, Dublin: Columba Press.

Morwood, Michael (2013) *It's Time: Challenges to the Doctrine of the Faith*, Kelmor Publications.

Ó Murchú, Diarmuid (2017) *Incarnation. A New Evolutionary Threshold*, New York, NY: Orbis Books.

Ó Murchú, Diarmuid (2019) *When the Disciple Comes of Age: Christian Identity in the 21st Century*, New York, NY: Orbis Books.

Rohr, Richard (2019) *The Universal Christ: How a Forgotten Reality Can Change Everything We See, Hope for and Believe*, Colorado Springs, CO: Convergent Books.

Treston, Kevin (2016) *Who Do You Say I Am? The Christ Story in the Cosmic Context*, Melbourne: Morning Star Publishing.